100ESSENTIAL**BLUES** GUITAR INTROS

Learn 100 Classic Intro Licks in the Style of the Blues Guitar Greats

STUART**RYAN**

FUNDAMENTAL**CHANGES**

100 Essential Blues Guitar Intros

Learn 100 Classic Intro Licks in the Style of the Blues Guitar Greats

ISBN: 978-1-78933-247-6

Published by **www.fundamental-changes.com**

Copyright © 2021 Stuart Ryan & Joseph Alexander

Edited by Tim Pettingale

www.fundamental-changes.com

Over 13,000 fans on Facebook: **FundamentalChangesInGuitar**

Instagram: **FundamentalChanges**

For over 350 Free Guitar Lessons with Videos Check Out

www.fundamental-changes.com

Cover Image Copyright: Shutterstock – Robert Kirby

Contents

Introduction

Simply starting a song can be one of the hardest things to get right on a blues gig, and the intro to a song can make or break the whole performance. Overplay and things may fall apart; don't say enough and you can lose the attention of the audience and the power of the band.

The great blues players are all masters at starting a song. Sometimes the intro might be a short, four-bar phrase, and at other times an extended solo jam that goes on for minutes before the song actually begins. What every great intro has in common, however, is the ability to grab your attention immediately, and convey the mood of what is to come – whether that's a powerful shuffle or a slow 12/8 groove.

Playing an intro is different to playing a solo. More often than not, an intro will need to be concise and melodic, with a defined beginning and end. There isn't always time for a big crescendo, and sometimes you need to say everything in just a few notes.

The intro licks in this book are inspired by a collection of the greatest blues players ever to have lived. Get them under your fingers and you will be better prepared to learn their solos and play in their style. You can learn them as written, or adapt them into different settings to increase your vocabulary. If you analyse them, you'll see how, in just a few bars, they say everything that needs to be said. Some players outline the chord changes, others go on brief (or wild) flights of fancy. Others practice restraint, knowing that the vocals are about to enter.

Of course, you may *not* be the one who opens the track – perhaps there is another guitarist or instrumentalist who takes that role – in which case, these licks can be used as intros to your *solos*. Sometimes, starting a solo is just as challenging as starting a song, so memorise these licks as "solo starters" that lead onto other ideas.

I hope these licks give you greater confidence when it comes to playing intros or starting solos. I remember all too well what it's like to stand there, count the band in, and just hope that you have enough ideas to hold it all together. Learn the examples in the book, jam with the backing tracks to improve your tone, touch and timing, then get out on a gig and go enjoy yourself!

Stu.

Get the Audio

The audio files for this book are available to download for free from **www.fundamental-changes.com.** The link is in the top right-hand corner. Simply select this book title from the drop-down menu and follow the instructions to get the audio.

We recommend that you download the files directly to your computer, not to your tablet, and extract them there before adding them to your media library. You can then put them on your tablet, iPod or burn them to CD. On the download page there is a help PDF and we also provide technical support via the contact form.

For over 350 free lessons with videos check out:

www.fundamental-changes.com

Join our active Facebook community:

www.facebook.com/groups/fundamentalguitar

Tag us for a share on Instagram: **FundamentalChanges**

Chapter One: Big Band Style Intros

This first set of examples don't copy any one artist in particular. Instead, they are reminiscent of the big, show-stopping blues style where the guitar is at the front of a large rhythm section. They're all about playing with big tone and conviction. Think B.B. King, or Gary Moore during the era when his expanded band included a full horn section.

It's common to play an unaccompanied lick as the intro to a blues song before the rhythm section enters. Don't underestimate how daunting this can be! You have to set the the mood and dynamic for the whole band, so whether you start subtlely or aggressively it's likely that the band will follow. For that reason, it's important to imagine the feel of the piece and how you need to set it up. It's essential that you nail the tempo (ask the drummer to give you a count-in if you're not sure) and ensure your phrase starts at the right point in the bar.

An overdriven tone will help create a good result and allow you to sustain notes more easily, but experiment with different tones to see how they force you to play different ideas. Blues is a nuanced language, so it's really important that you listen to each audio track while learning the examples. If you haven't already done so, download the free audio from **www.fundamental-changes.com** It'll make the following lines much easier to master. That said, let's dive straight into the examples.

The first example fuses the A Minor and A Major pentatonic scales with the A Blues scale to create a varied, melodic sound built around changing just one or two notes in a phrase. In bar two, the hammer-on from the minor to major 3rd (C to C#) on the G string is typical of the minor/major duality of the blues.

The muted rake across the strings at the start of bar four is a great phrasing device to make a note pop out. To execute it, lightly rest the first finger across the D and G strings to mute them while you hold down the 10th fret with the third finger. Now brush the pick across all three strings and hear how the final note jumps out!

Example 1a

The next lick also blends A Minor and Major pentatonic scales. It opens with a rhythmic phrase that is trickier than it looks on paper, requiring you to play a group of four notes over the underlying triplet feel. Once you hear it, however, you'll get it, so listen to the audio first to get the sound in your head. To make the whole tone bends in bars two and four easier to play, and avoid finger strain, make sure you bend the notes with your third finger, supported by first and second fingers. This will give you maximum stability and accuracy.

Example 1b

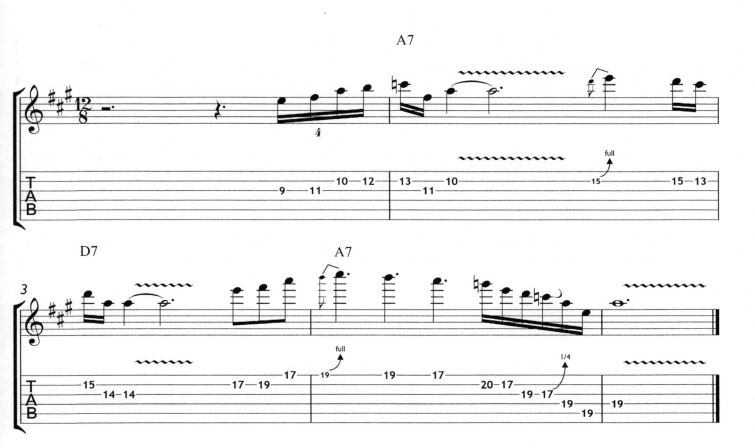

Based around the A Minor Pentatonic scale, Example 1c is a more restrained idea. It'll sound best with a singing, overdriven tone with lots of sustain. Bar three starts at the 9th fret of the G string with the colourful interval of a 9th (E) over the D7 chord. Don't forget to focus on the rhythmic elements here too, as you contrast the triplet feel in bar one with another "four against three" rhythm at the end of bar two. The latter adds to the laid back feel of the phrasing.

Example 1c

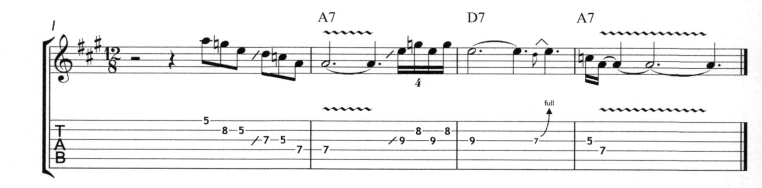

The main challenge of the next lick is the string skip that follows the bend in bar one. Use your third finger to play the bend from the 16th fret on the G string and have your first finger ready, prepared to play the 14th fret of the high E string. Adding larger intervallic jumps like this to your licks will immediately give them a fresher sound and help you to break out of clichéd patterns.

Repeating the first three notes from bar one in bar two highlights another useful deivce – *repetition*. Tasteful use of repetition will make your licks sound more melodic, consistent and planned.

Example 1d

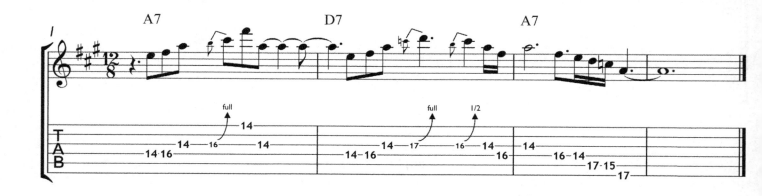

Often, less is more. Can you play a simple two-note phrase for a whole bar? Of course you can! Floating over the tripet feel groove, the two-note idea of bar one creates a tension that is released in bar two. To contrast with this dramatic opening, the rest of the lick is much more sparse. The line derives from the A Minor Pentatonic scale, but the phrasing and melody bring it to life. Play the B string bends in bar three with the third finger, with first and second fingers supporting, as before.

Example 1e

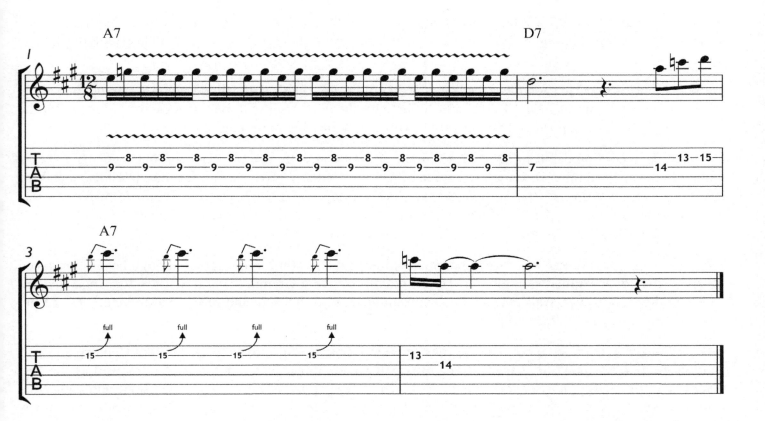

In the chapters that follow, we'll begin to look at the approaches of some of the all-time great blues players.

Chapter Two: T-Bone Walker

Aaron Thibeaux "T-Bone" Walker, was born in 1910 in Texas, USA. As a youth, Walker learned to play several instruments including piano, violin, banjo and ukulele, as both of his parents (and his stepfather), were musicians.

Walker began his musical career as a teenager. His family were friends with Blind Lemon Jefferson, one of the most popular blues artists of the 1920s, and Jefferson influenced Walker to pursue a career in music. By the age of 15, Walker was a professional performer working on the Southern blues circuit.

He made his recording debut in 1929 for Columbia Records and, by age 25, was working regularly in clubs around Los Angeles both as a singer and guitarist. By the 1940s, Walker was performing in Chicago and his best-known composition, *Call It Stormy Monday (But Tuesday Is Just as Bad)* – commonly known as *Stormy Monday* – dates from this period. Much of his best-known work was undertaken in the late 1940s–50s while he recorded for Black and White Records, Imperial Records and the Atlantic label.

By the early 1960s, Walker was experiencing a commercial downturn in his career, though he still produced several critically acclaimed solo albums. He eventually earned a Grammy award in 1971 for *Good Feelin'*. By the mid-70s, however, Walker was suffering from increasing ill health and suffered a stroke in 1974 before sadly passing away in 1975, aged just 64.

T-Bone Walker is heralded as one of the most influential blues guitar players of the 20th Century and was admired by players including Chuck Berry, B.B. King and Jimi Hendrix. He is widely viewed as the first notable electric blues guitarist and was a great showman when playing live. Many of the stage acrobatics that Chuck Berry, and later Jimi Hendrix, would indulge in were directly drawn from Walker's own live routines, such as playing the guitar behind his back and playing with his teeth.

Several of Walker's songs have been recorded by well-known rock and blues artists. Most notably, *Stormy Monday* was covered by Bobby Bland, The Allman Brothers on their 1971 live album *At Fillmore East* album, Cream on their Royal Albert Hall live album and countless others. Walker's legacy is still celebrated every year in Texas through the T-Bone Walker Blues Festival.

Walker was associated principally with early Gibson hollow-body guitars, starting with the ES-250, then later the ES-5 and ES-335 models, when Gibson's production of semi-hollow guitars expanded. For amplifiers, he generally favoured a clean tone from either an early Gibson EH-130 or a Fender 4x10 Bassman combo.

T-Bone Walker's use of the blues scale influenced many later rock and blues guitarists and he sometimes included elements of jazz in his playing. When light-gauge strings became widely available he began to explore the wide-interval string bending that has become a staple of modern blues guitar.

Walker is often credited with bringing electric blues guitar to public attention as a legitimate solo instrument, rather than it being restricted solely to a rhythm role.

Recommended Listening

Complete Imperial Recordings 1950-1954

T-Bone Blues

Good Feelin'

Every Day I Have the Blues

Here is Walker's famous swing feel and use of triplets in action. This lick uses the G Minor Pentatonic scale throughout and the challenge is to nail the whole tone bends on the G string. Wrap your thumb over the top of the neck for stability and reinforce the third finger bend with your first and second fingers. Note how much space is used in this lick. One reason for that will become clear in the next prhase and it's a great tactic to adopt.

Example 2a

T-Bone's amps didn't have much sustain, so he could either leave space between his licks as in the previous example or weave long, flowing bebop-style jazz lines. Use the one-finger-per-fret rule to play through bars 1-2, with the first finger assigned to the 3rd fret. In bar three, the third finger is a good option for the notes on the G string, followed by the second finger on the B string.

Example 2b

These rich G9 chords are a great alternative to starting with licks. Omitting the root note of the chord helps it cut through, giving the sound more clarity, as well as making it easier to play. Barre the notes on the G, B and E strings with your third or fourth finger and use the first finger for the note on the D string. Strum the chords lightly and, after each strum, quickly release the pressure on the fretting hand fingers to get the correct sound.

Example 2c

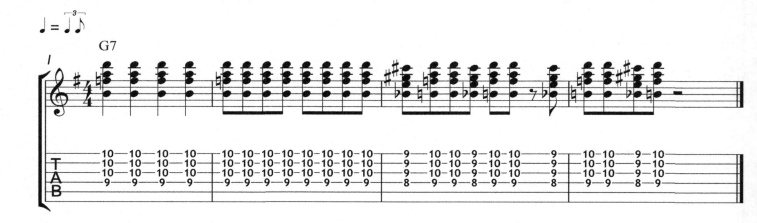

There are two uses of repetition in the next lick. The opening phrase is repeated over the first two bars, plus in bar three each note is played twice. To play the double-stop phrase in bar three, rest a first finger barre over the G and B strings at the 3rd fret, then use the second finger to quickly hammer-on to the 4th fret of the G string.

Example 2d

Sliding into a double-stop is a subtle but important phrasing tool, used here in bar two. You can hear the influence of Chuck Berry's *Johnny B. Goode*. Fret the double-stop with your first finger then quickly slide up to it from a fret below. You need to hit the 3rd fret at the start of each beat. Accent the first note of each triplet by hitting the strings a little harder each time. This phrase moves from G Major Pentatonic in bars 1-2 to G Dorian and G Major Pentatonic in the following bars.

Example 2e

Chapter Three: B.B. King Part One

Riley Benjamin "B.B." King was born in 1925 in Mississippi, USA and is one the most influential and commercially successful blues musicians of all time. The son of sharecroppers, he was raised by his grandmother after his parents separated. His first musical experience was as a member of a Gospel choir.

King's interest in guitar seems to have begun around the age of 12 years old, when he acquired his first guitar. He became interested in the blues music he heard on the radio and by the late 1940's he was performing regularly and building an enthusiastic following.

By 1949, King had signed a record deal with RPM Records and also assembled his own band, The B.B. King Review. King's reputation as a guitar player, singer and composer was well established by the 1950s and he had a string of successful hits singles during the decade such as *Sweet Little Angel* and *Every Day I Have the Blues*. These singles helped him achieve great commercial success and he toured almost constantly.

By the 1960s, King was a well-established and successful blues musician with considerable popularity, and the British blues boom of the mid-1960s helped to keep him in the public eye on a world stage. B.B. King also undertook a support tour with The Rolling Stones in 1969 which gained him much visibility with a new, mostly white, rock audience. In 1970, his song *The Thrill Is Gone* won a Grammy award.

King was one of the hardest working blues musicians of his generation, regularly performing 300 dates a year and continuing to do so almost up to his passing in 2015. King collaborated with many other artists during his long career (including U2 on the single *When Love Comes to Town* in 1988). He appeared in several films and was a regular TV guest. Virtually every modern-day blues guitarist has been influenced by King's playing and song writing, with *Rolling Stone* magazine ranking him number 6 on their list of *The 100 Greatest Guitarists of All Time*.

B.B. King's playing style is instantly recognisable, characterised by a rich, singing vibrato which has been copied by many other guitarists. Mostly utilising blues and Pentatonic scales, his playing, especially his phrasing, is extremely vocal in nature, undoubtedly influenced by his wonderful talent as a singer. King rarely played chords; instead his guitar playing was mostly used to support his singing.

Spend some time on B.B.'s playing and you'll learn how phrasing, vibrato and restraint can shape a great blues lick. His ethos always appeared to be, "Don't say more than you have to, leave them wanting more" (or perhaps "Don't outstay your welcome!") and his hook-laden intro phrases are perfect examples of this.

Although King used a Fender Esquire early in his career, he is best known for his use of the Gibson ES-355 which he affectionately named Lucille. In 1980, the Gibson company launched a B.B. King Lucille model and in 2005 manufactured a limited run of 80 special-edition versions to celebrate King's 80th birthday.

King favoured amplifiers that produced a clean, clear sound, and was a long-time user of a Lab Series L5 2x12 that was popular with a number of guitarists in the late '70s and '80s but is no longer manufactured.

B.B. King occasionally used a Fender Twin Reverb amplifier but rarely (if ever) used effects on his guitar tone, with any required tonal changes coming from his fingers and the instrument itself.

Recommended Listening

Singin' the Blues

Live at the Regal

Live in Cook County Jail

Riding with the King

This lick demonstrates how a simple B Minor Pentatonic scale can do (almost) all of the work for you if you add some contrast in rhythm and space. The "blues curl" bend featured here was at the heart of much of B.B.'s vocabulary. The first blues curl appears at the start of bar two, where your first finger will gently bend the E string at the 7th fret. Experiment with how far you push the string, as unlike half or whole tone bends, quarter tone bends are less of a precise art and your ear will be the judge of when it's right. Repeat this idea in bar two on the G string.

Example 3a

This example contains a great B.B. lesson: you don't have to start on beat 1! It's all about the phrasing with this B Minor Pentatonic idea. Look out for the pre-bend on beat 3 in bar one. Accurately pre-bend the 9th fret of the G string up a whole step (two frets) before you strike the string and quickly release it. The third finger is the best choice here. Notice how B.B. liked to move out of position on the E string when building his phrases.

Example 3b

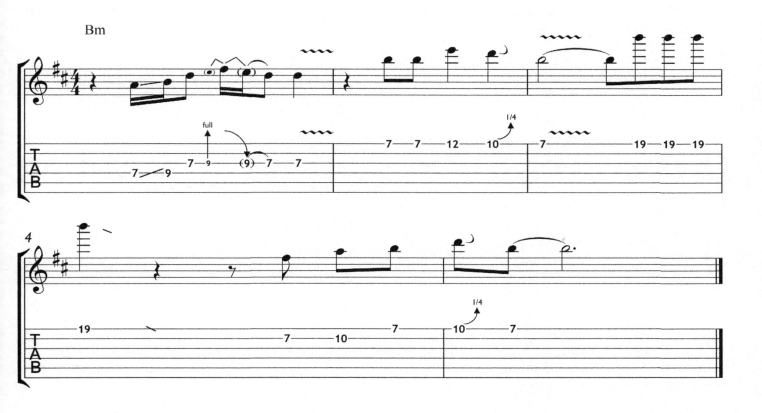

The next lick contrasts space with brief rapid-fire phrases. The ideas are focused on the E and B strings around the 10th and 12th frets and draw again from B Minor Pentatonic. Working on just two strings like this forces us to think harder about our phrasing and keeps us from falling into stale patterns. Always be aware of the notes you play, and notice in this phrase that we keep targeting the B root note at the 12th fret.

Example 3c

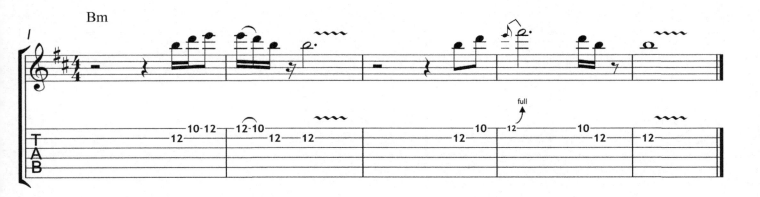

All the B.B.-isms come together in the next lick. There are licks played over two strings, the blues curl and his use of sustained notes and space. At the start of bar three use your third or fourth finger for the note on the 10th fret and remember that bending fingers should usually be reinforced, even when they are just going for a quarter tone blues curl.

Example 3d

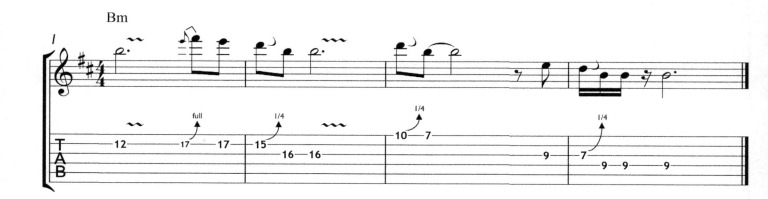

Here is another idea that focuses mainly on two strings. Moving between positions on just two strings forces us to seek out those all important root/third/fifth chord tones and prevents us from meandering around or getting lost in the pentatonic box shape.

Example 3e

Chapter Four: B.B. King Part Two

You've just learned how B.B. King might introduce a slow, minor ballad, but the next set of examples show how he might introduce a slow 12/8 groove.

While B.B.King was well known for playing on a minor blues, with beautiful, soft dynamics, he was just as much a master on swing and shuffles too. Listen to his classic 1964 album *Live At The Regal Theater* and you'll hear all these facets of his playing.

This first lick begins with the classic minor to major 3rd move on the G string, followed by a challenging rhythmic phrase where four notes are played evenly against the underlying triplet feel on beat 4. Listen to the audio for reference. One of the harder aspects of B.B.'s style is his ability to play great vibrato with his first finger, such as at the start of bar two on the 8th fret of the B string. Relax the fretting hand, then apply the vibrato with the first finger, aiming for a wide/rapid shaking of the note. From bar two the lick uses the C Major Pentatonic scale before moving briefly to C Minor Pentatonic over the F7 chord.

Example 4a

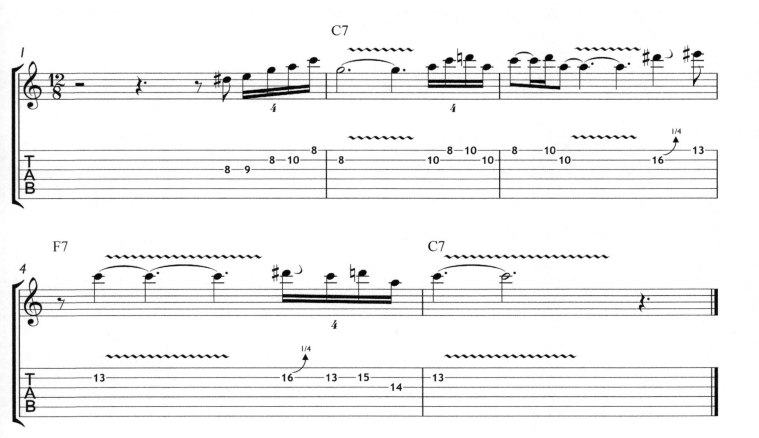

This lick again demonstrates B.B.'s ability to seamlessly move between minor and major pentatonic scale ideas within the same phrase. Aim for a lazy, behind the beat feel and have the fretting hand ready for those position shifts up and down the B and E strings. Practice your first finger vibrato on the E and B strings throughout.

Example 4b

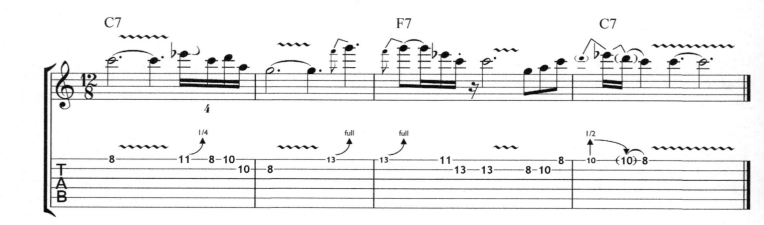

The challenge in this lick is to not play on beat 1 of the bar for most of it. Timing the placement of your intro phrases is a great skill to develop and you'll learn a lot from listening to where and how blues masters like B.B. King began and ended their phrases.

Example 4c

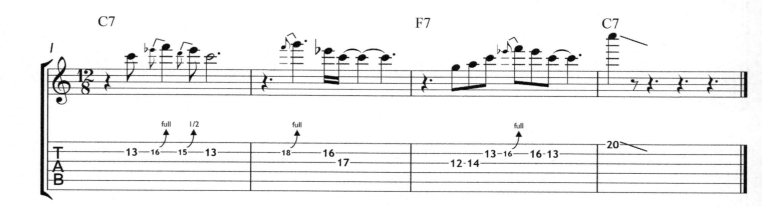

This lick demonstrates how using rhythm and phrasing can transform a simple C Minor Pentatonic lick into a strong melodic idea – in this instance by incorporating quarter tone bends and playing with a four-against-three feel. Bar one starts in the familiar C Minor Pentatonic box at the 8th fret before shifting position to the 13th fret. In bar two, it's tempting to play the first bend with the fourth finger but I'd recommend using the third finger for the bends at both the 16th and 15th frets.

Example 4d

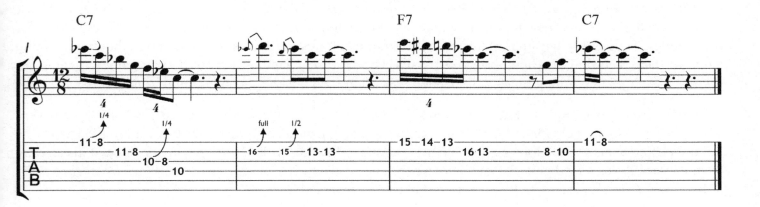

Always think about the direction of the notes you're playing – are you ascending or descending? You can literally see the "shape" of this lick in the notation, ascending and descending the C Minor Pentatonic scale to create melodic movement and contrast. In bar one, use the fourth finger for the 10th fret and first finger for the 7th fret, to get your hand in the right position. Use the second finger for the slide into the 9th fret and the first finger on the 8th fret at the end of the bar.

Example 4e

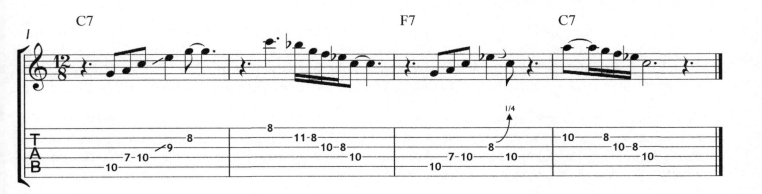

Chapter Five: Eric Clapton

Born in Surrey, England, in 1945, Eric Patrick Clapton is one of the most recognised electric blues and rock guitarists in the world. He began playing guitar around the age of 13, when he was given an acoustic guitar for his birthday. He quickly became infatuated with American blues musicians, often spending hours practicing along to their recordings to hone his guitar skills. By the time Clapton was 16, he had gained a name for himself as an up-and-coming blues guitarist and was often seen busking in and around London.

After performing in a number of different bands he was invited to join The Yardbirds in 1963. The group were a rock and roll band, heavily influenced by the blues, and Clapton remained with them until 1965 when he left to become a member of John Mayall's Blues Breakers. Playing with Mayall further developed his already formidable skills as a lead guitarist and he recorded one of his most acclaimed albums, *Blues Breakers – John Mayall with Eric Clapton* (sometimes referred to as the Beano album).

In July 1966, Clapton joined forces with bassist Jack Bruce and drummer Ginger Baker to form Cream, one of the earliest rock super-groups. They quickly rose to superstardom before disbanding just a few years later. After Cream, Clapton played with Blind Faith and Derek and the Dominoes (producing the classic *Layla* album) before entering a reclusive period that was sadly marred by drug addiction. He re-emerged in the mid-1970s with many successful solo albums, and by the 1980s was producing more commercial recordings than he had in the '70s.

A long battle with alcohol and personal problems was eventually overcome and by the 1990s Clapton's career had become more consistent and successful in terms of musical output. The tragic death of his son Conor in 1991 inspired the song *Tears in Heaven* which became a major commercial success, as was his *Unplugged* album which remains one of his biggest-selling albums to date.

Clapton's steady touring and recording continued into the 2000s, and he has recently returned to his blues roots, paying tribute to his influencers such as Robert Johnson. Clapton remains one of the most influential blues and rock guitarists to this day and has received numerous Grammy awards. In 1998 he founded the Crossroads Centre in Antigua for drug addiction and was awarded the CBE in 2004 for his services to music.

His lead guitar style is clearly influenced by the blues and he predominantly uses pentatonic and blues scales in his soloing. Influenced by guitarists such as Buddy Guy, Freddie King and B.B. King, among many others, Clapton's approach is much copied by modern players. He has a particularly expressive vibrato technique and frequently uses string bending to great effect in his solos.

Eric Clapton has been associated with several different guitar models over his career, most notably the Gibson Les Paul Standard in his early work and the Gibson SG and ES-335 for a period with Cream. Since the early 1970s he has commonly played Stratocasters and Fender eventually produced a signature model for him.

Marshall amplifiers were Clapton's mainstay from the mid-1960s onwards, especially with Cream where he became one of the first guitarists to use stacked amplifiers and 4x12 cabinets. He switched over to using smaller (and generally lower wattage amps) by Fender and Music Man in the 1970s, and for the most part has remained with this setup.

Clapton isn't especially associated with any effects units but has made effective use of the wah-wah pedal in some of his recordings. He generally avoids heavily effected guitar tones, preferring to keep to a simple setup.

Recommended Listening

John Mayall's Blues Breakers with Eric Clapton – John Mayall

E.C. Was Here

Me and Mr Johnson

From the Cradle

The first example shows how Clapton serves the song with a restrained, melodic intro based on the A Minor Pentatonic scale. It takes a "busy/sparse" approach to the playing that creates a call and response idea. Start off with the third finger at the 9th fret and the second finger at the 8th fret. At the end of bar two, strike the note at the 9th fret then immediately slide down to the 7th fret; the first note here should only sound very briefly.

Example 5a

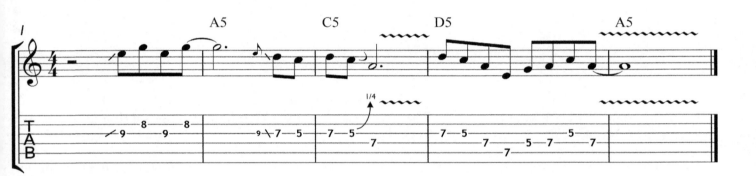

Small position shifts are the key feature of this A Minor Pentatonic scale idea. Sliding from the 14th fret to the 12th fret may be a small leap but accuracy is critical – go one fret too far and it all falls apart! Similarly, sliding into the 12th fret in bars 3-4 needs clinical precision. Although there is no indication of where you slide from, it's generally safe to assume that fretting two frets higher then sliding into the target note will work well.

Example 5b

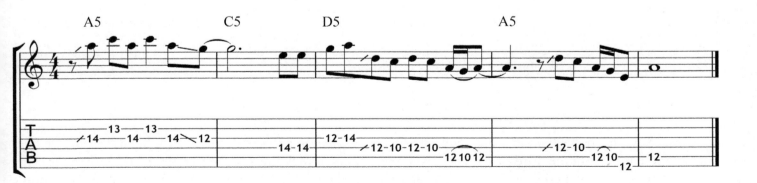

We know that phrasing is a vital component of the Blues (bends, slides, legato etc), but it's not necessary to use *all* those devices together. Often Clapton lets the melody do the work with barely any phrasing. Long sustained notes are made easier by his thick, chewy overdriven tone.

Play the repeating double-stop in bar three with the second finger on the G string and third finger on the D string. This will make the transition easier when you replace the third finger with the first, to slide from the 12th to 14th fret into the final note of the lick.

Example 5c

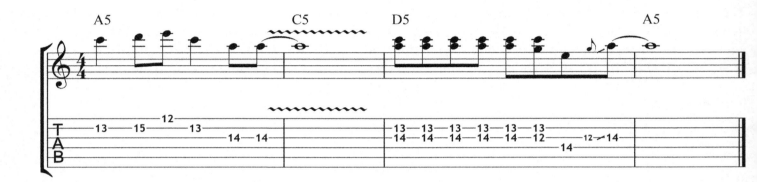

Here's an example of Clapton's more aggressive blues/rock style, similar to that found on tracks like *Crossroads*. The use of the dotted 1/8th note on beat 2 of bar two, followed by a 1/16th note creates a rhythm that was a real feature of this era.

In bar three, keep the first finger barred at the 17th fret throughout. Use the second finger for the hammer-on at the 18th fret and the third finger for the notes on the 19th/20th frets.

Example 5d

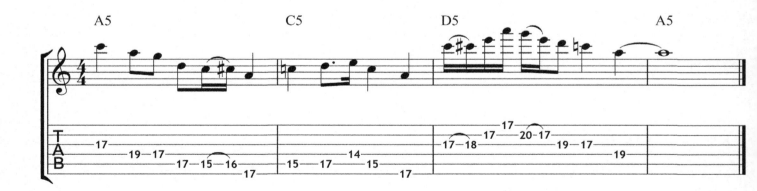

This last example shows the more challenging aspects of Clapton's playing. In bar two, bend the note on beat 1 up a whole tone with the third finger and sustain it while you pick the 15th fret on the E string (beat 2). This is followed by re-picking the sustained bend, so it sounds the pitch at the 17th fret. Bar three shows Clapton's exciting control of fast triplet rhythms. Use the first and third fingers for the pull-offs on the B and E strings.

Example 5e

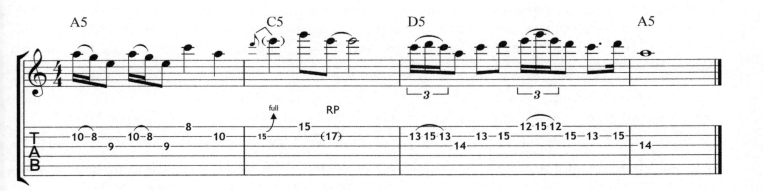

Chapter Six: Freddie King

Freddie King was born in September 1934 and raised in Gilmer, Texas, where he was taught how to play the guitar as a 6-year-old by his mother and uncle. King played acoustic blues at first, much in the style of players like Lightin' Hopkins, but by the time he was a teenager he had gravitated to the raw electric tones of the Chicago Blues style.

At the age of 16, his family moved to Chicago, where he frequented local music clubs, listening to popular blues musicians such as Muddy Waters, Jimmy Rogers, Robert Lockwood Jr., Little Walter and Eddie Taylor. Inspired by these artists, King formed his own band, The Every Hour Blues Boys and began performing live.

By the mid-1950s, King was playing on records for Parrott and Chess Records, as well as performing with Earle Payton's Blues Cats and the Little Sonny Cooper Band. King's first solo recording was in 1957 when he recorded Country Boy for the small independent label El-Bee. The single, however, was not a commercial success and gained little public attention.

In 1960, King signed with Federal Records and recorded his first single for the label, *You've Got to Love Her with a Feeling*. The single appeared in September of 1960 and became a minor hit in early 1961. This was followed by the instrumental *Hide Away*, the composition that would become King's most influential recording. It was adapted by King and Magic Sam from an original Hound Dog Taylor instrumental and named after one of the most popular bars in Chicago. It was released as the B-side of *I Love the Woman* in the fall of 1961 and became a major hit, reaching number five on the R&B charts. *Hide Away* was later covered by Eric Clapton (with John Mayall), and Stevie Ray Vaughan.

King's first full-length solo album, *Freddy King Sings*, was released in 1961, and followed later that year by *Let's Hide Away* and *Dance Away with Freddy King: Strictly Instrumental*. In 1961, he recorded another series of blues instrumentals, including *San-Ho-Zay, The Stumble* and *I'm Tore Down*, each of which are blues classics and have been covered by artists such as Magic Sam, Stevie Ray Vaughan, Dave Edmunds and Peter Green.

King's influence was heard throughout the blues and rock boom of the mid-late 1960s, most notably when Eric Clapton made King's *Hide Away* his showcase instrumental with John Mayall in 1965.

King signed with the Atlantic/Cotillion label in 1968, releasing *Freddie King is a Blues Master* the following year, and *My Feeling for the Blues* in 1970.

In 1974, he signed a contract with the Robert Stigwood Organisation (RSO), Eric Clapton's record label at the time, and released *Burglar*, which was produced and recorded with Clapton. King toured America, Europe and Australia and released his second RSO album, *Larger Than Life*, in 1975.

King kept up a 300-date-per-year schedule and, despite poor health due to his diet, embarked on a tour of America in 1976. Sadly, he died in December that year of pancreatitis at the age of 42.

Known as one of the "Three 'Kings" of the blues, alongside B.B. King and Albert King, Freddie was considered one of the most influential guitar players of his generation. "The Texas Cannonball" was not only known for his guitar playing, but also for his powerful voice and compositional talent. King was also one of the first blues performers to employ a multi-racial band.

King's guitar style was an amalgam of Texas-influenced open string blues patterns and Chicago-style pentatonic runs and string bends. He played both with a pick and with his fingers and often used the latter to vary the dynamics of his playing. He also used finger and thumb picks to achieve a more aggressive attack on the instrument.

King's playing influenced many rock and blues players during the 1960s–70s, including artists such as Eric Clapton and Peter Green, and his compositions are still played by contemporary blues musicians like Joe Bonamassa and Walter Trout.

King's favoured instrument early in his career was a Gibson Les Paul Gold Top with P-90 single-coil pickups, although he later switched to a Gibson ES-335 fitted with humbuckers. He used Gibson amplifiers such as the GA-40 and later Fender tube combos such as the Quad Reverb and Dual Showman with the volume and treble settings turned up full.

One crucial point is that he used a thunbpick and a metal fingerpick on his first finger rather than a plectrum. Playing like this changes the tone and attack and it's well worth experimenting with Freddie's unorthodox approach. However, you can get in the tonal ballpark by just using a metal plectrum.

Recommended Listening

Burglar

Let's Hide Away and Dance Away with Freddie King

Gives You a Bonanza of Instrumentals

Just Pickin'

After a sparse opening phrase, the emphasis is on aggression in this first example, with some technical challenges in bar three. The phrase in bar three comprises a rapid bend, release, and pull-off sequence that repeats. Use the third finger for the 17th fret bend with the first finger resting behind it on the 15th fret, ready to execute the pull-off. The second and third fingers alternate on the 16th and 17th frets of the G string.

Example 6a

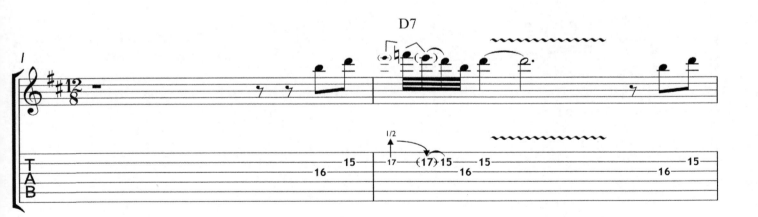

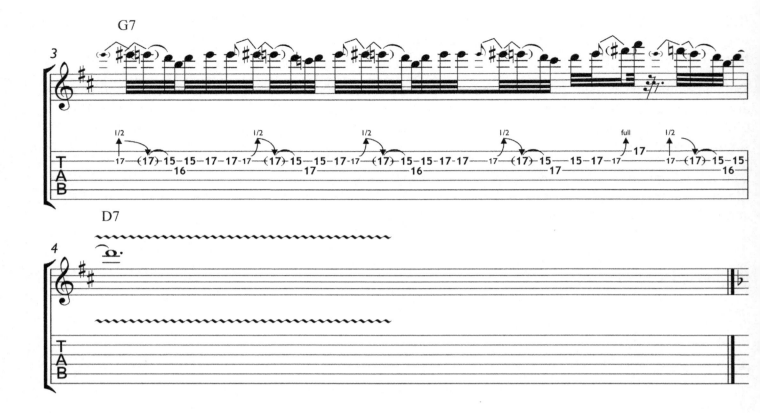

The next Freddie-style lick bounces between D Major and Minor pentatonic scales. Pay careful attention to nailing the wide variety of rhythms in this phrase. Start very slowly and remember to reinforce all the string bends with fingers behind the fretted note.

Example 6b

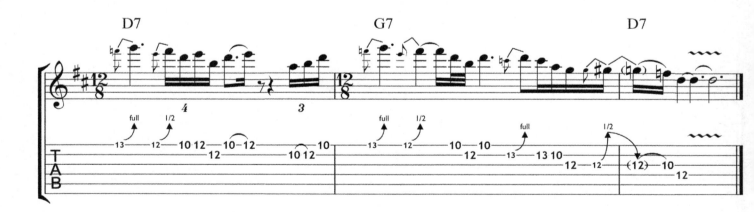

The next example contrasts the previous rhythmic challenges with a more measured, melodic phrase. Check out the targeting of chord tones throughout. Aiming for the root, third or fifth of a chord is a great way to start a phrase or sit on one note for a while, such as in bar two, where the fifth of the G7 chord at the 15th fret on the B string is sustained. You can use the third and first fingers all the way through but shift position down in the second half so that your first finger plays the 10th fret.

Example 6c

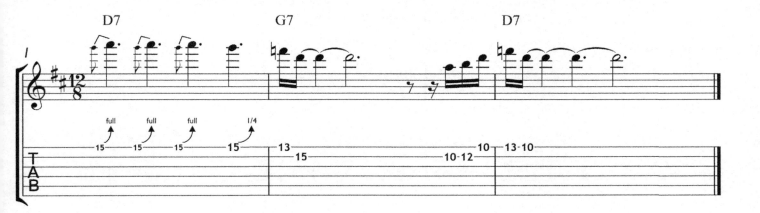

The use of repetition is always helpful when it comes to creating a melodic hook, as in the next example. The third and first fingers take care of note duties here. Be sure to release the whole step bend quickly, so you can play the G note on the 15th fret cleanly.

Example 6d

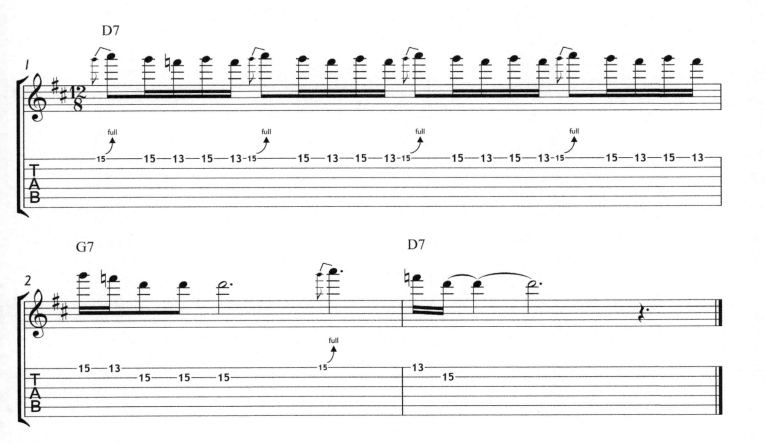

Interval jumps between notes yield great melodic ideas. In this example, moving from the 10th fret of the B string to the 13th fret of the E string provides a change from the typical, smaller blues intervals of thirds and seconds. This phrase extends the D Minor Pentatonic scale by adding the ninth (E) at the 12th fret on the first string and the thirteenth (B) at the 12th fret on the second string.

Example 6e

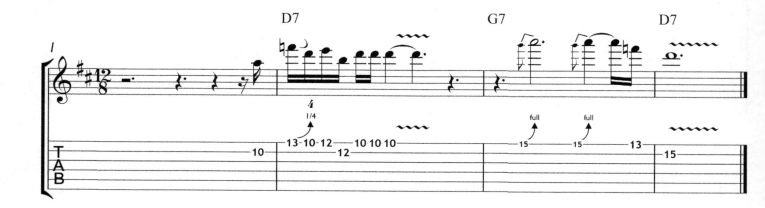

Chapter Seven: Joe Bonamassa Part One

Joseph Leonard Bonamassa was born on the 8th May, 1977, in New Hartford, New York. His musical talent was noticed at a young age. Having begun his guitar journey at the age of just four, he was playing Stevie Ray Vaughan songs by the age of seven. He was mentored by guitarist Danny Gatton from the age of 11, and when he was 12, formed his own band called Smokin' Joe Bonamassa, which gigged around western New York and Pennsylvania. Bonamassa was also invited to play with B.B. King around the same time.

Bonamassa began his own recording career in the early 1990s with a band called Bloodlines, which featured several high-profile rock offspring (including Berry Oakley Jr., son of Berry Oakley, bassist for the Allman Brothers, Waylon Krieger, son of Robby Krieger the guitarist of The Doors, Aaron Hagar, son of Sammy Hagar, and Miles Davis' son, Erin). Their debut album, 1994's *Bloodline,* was a fusion of blues, funk, boogie and rock. High profile opening slots followed on tours with Buddy Guy, Foreigner, George Thorogood, Robert Cray, Stephen Stills, Joe Cocker and Gregg Allman, among many others.

Bonamassa's debut solo album, *A New Day Yesterday,* was a surprisingly mature, well-rounded recording for a 23-year-old and received considerable critical acclaim. The album reached number 9 on the Billboard Blues chart. Bonamassa's talents remained largely confined to the US for a time, but with a growing base of admirers from the worlds of both blues and rock, his commercial success grew quickly and he began rapidly selling out tours. In 2007, *Sloe Gin* (his seventh studio album) would finally bring him international success.

Sloe Gin received heavy airplay on Planet Rock throughout 2007 and the album climbed into the UK album charts on the back of favourable reviews from fans who saw him on his UK tour. In 2008, the *Live from Nowhere in Particular* album saw further success for Bonamassa (particularly in the UK), peaking at number 45 in the album charts – a rare achievement for a blues guitarist.

In 2010, with his new studio album, *The Ballad of John Henry*, and a highly-acclaimed performance at the Royal Albert Hall, lasting commercial success arrived for Bonamassa. His next studio release, *Black Rock* was his highest charting solo studio album. 2010 also saw Bonamassa play more than 200 gigs and form the group *Black Country Communion* with Glenn Hughes, Jason Bonham and Derek Sherinian.

In 2011, Bonamassa released *Dust Bowl*, followed by a second album with BCC, and an album called *Don't Explain* with blues singer Beth Hart – all while keeping up a lengthy touring schedule.

Bonamassa has a distinct, modern guitar tone and usually plays a signature Gibson Les Paul. He has a refined guitar technique and is arguably amongst the best technicians in the modern blues idiom. He can readily replicate both classic and modern playing styles and, unlike older generation blues players, he uses dramatic alternate-picked rock lines and arpeggios.

You can't talk about Joe Bonamassa without discussing his fantastic tone. Growing up around a father who was a guitar dealer, it should come as no surprise that Joe is a gear collector. The extent of his collection is quite staggering and he has pretty much one (or more) of everything. He famously has three vintage 'burst Les Pauls and a huge array of signature equipment, from Gibson Les Pauls to 335s and more, to a limited run Fender Custom Shop Telecaster. He seems most at home with a Les Paul and humbuckers are certainly part of the key to getting his huge, British influenced sound.

Amp-wise, he has used a number of different brands over the years, from current production models to rare, sought-after vintage pieces. A fan of amp gain over pedals, he has used various Marshall, Budda, Fender Tweed and Dumble amplifiers. Like Kenny Wayne Shepherd, he runs several amps together and plays *very loud*, as anyone who has seen him in concert will testify. Joe's tone is on the dark side of things, so don't be afraid to roll back the treble on your amp or guitar when playing his licks. This preference most likely comes from listening to Clapton's early "woman" tone in his bluesbreakers era.

To Joe's credit, he takes all his valuable vintage gear on the road, so seeing him live is almost a history lesson in how good vintage gear is and how great it can sound in the right hands.

Recommended Listening

Blues Deluxe

Live from the Royal Albert Hall

Blues of Desperation

A New Day Yesterday

This first set of Bonamassa examples takes us back to a 12/8 groove with a minor feel. Note how minor pentatonic ideas are blended with the natural minor scale – a melodic way of playing the blues that hints at the influence of Gary Moore on Bonamassa's style. Also demonstrated here is Joe's complete control over the whole fretboard. While he plays within the familiar pentatonic box shapes, he can also easily create licks that use the whole range of the instrument.

Although the backing track for this chapter is quite slow, these intros are technically challenging due to the amount of notes Bonamassa typically crams into a short space of time. This is more akin to rock technique, so these intros may place some new demands on your picking and fretting hands. Persevere though, as working on material like this will pay dividends on all aspects of your playing. Be sure to keep both hands relaxed throughout to keep these lines flowing.

Bonamassa's use of the range of the neck to create long, flowing lines calls for some careful planning with fretting hand fingering and position shifts. This first lick is centred around the 3rd fret, so use the third and first fingers to play the opening phrase, then quickly shift position to use the third finger again at the 11th fret. A bigger jump is needed in bar four: start with the first finger at the 3rd fret, follow this with the third and second fingers at the 7th and 6th frets, then use the third finger again for the big bend at the 5th fret.

Example 7a

In the next example, straightforward licks using the G Natural Minor scale are interspersed with fast alternate picked lines, such as the sextuplet phrase in bar three. Play this fast run using the first and third fingers throughout. Execute a quick position shift to relocate the third finger at the 15th fret for the descending part of the line, to avoid a big stretch. Notice the use of a D# diminished seventh arpeggio over the D7 in bar four, which creates some jazz-style tension.

Example 7b

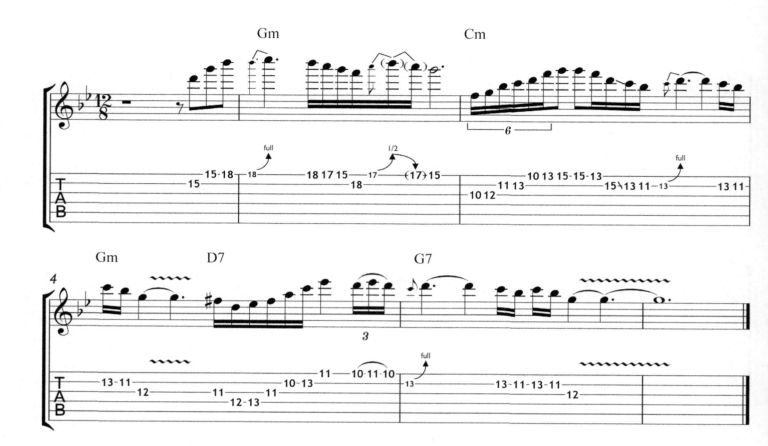

Joe is a master of restraint and melody too. This line begins with a simple, tasetful Gm to Gm7 arpeggio pattern. Bar three features a bluesy country-rock bend, so use the third finger to play the bend on the B string at the 13th fret (C to D) followed up by the fourth finger fretting the 13th fret on the E string. The aim is to keep these two notes ringing to create a country-style pedal steel sound.

Example 7c

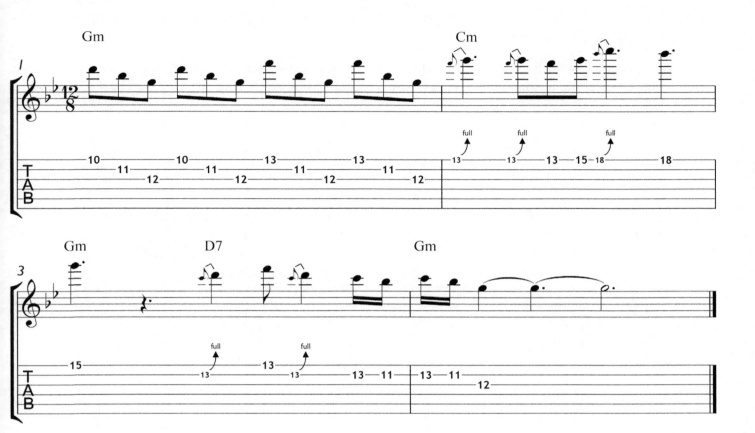

Here's a G Minor Pentatonic idea with a brief foray into G Natural Minor in bar two thanks to the Eb note on the 4th fret of the B string. Adding some natural minor harmony to your playing gives you a great colour that goes beyond pentatonic and blues scales. There are various ways to finger the double-stop here, but the third and second fingers on the G and B strings are a good choice, as you must quickly get to the 3rd fret with the first finger next.

Example 7d

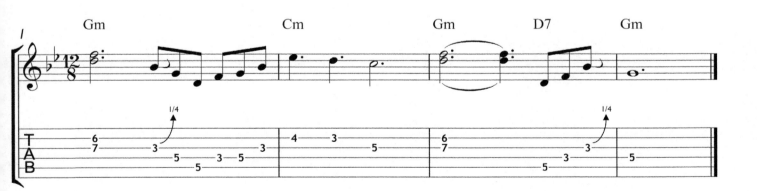

Octaves can be a great device to thicken up intro lines, but make sure to mute unwanted string noise, especially when playing with a lot of distortion. In bar one, use the first and fourth fingers to fret the octaves and rest the underside of the first finger over the G string to stop it from sounding. Repeat the process in bar three, this time fretting with the first and third fingers.

You'll hear on Joe's recordings that he sometimes takes this idea further by tremelo picking his octaves i.e. rapidly alternate picking to sound the notes as often as possible before moving on to the next part of the phrase.

Example 7e

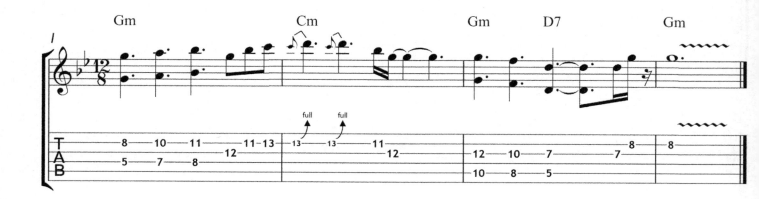

Chapter Eight: Joe Bonamassa Part Two

Joe Bonamassa has released a huge output of recorded material from studio albums to live recordings, so it's worth taking a look at another Bonamassa-style intro to see what more we can learn. This next set of examples looks at how Joe would play over a slow, moody blues in 4/4 time. You'll see again how his intros often combine restrained, melodic phrases with sudden bursts of technique. There are some great lessons to learn here, one of the most important being that it's very important to warm up fully before playing or performing!

While the slower licks pose challenges of phrasing and timing, it's the rapid-fire technical phrases that can really trip you up, so I recommend tackling these challenging sections in isolation. Use them technical exercises to improve your speed, co-ordination and alternate picking.

In Example 8a, starting with two bends on the G string in quick succession calls for control and accuracy. The third finger will be doing the fretting work here and, as always, back it up with the first and second fingers supporting.

Bar four features typical Joe speed alternate picking. Slow this section down and work on your fretting/picking hand coordination, building up the speed gradually. Play the 13th fret with the first finger, the 15th with the second finger, and the 17th with the fourth finger.

Example 8a

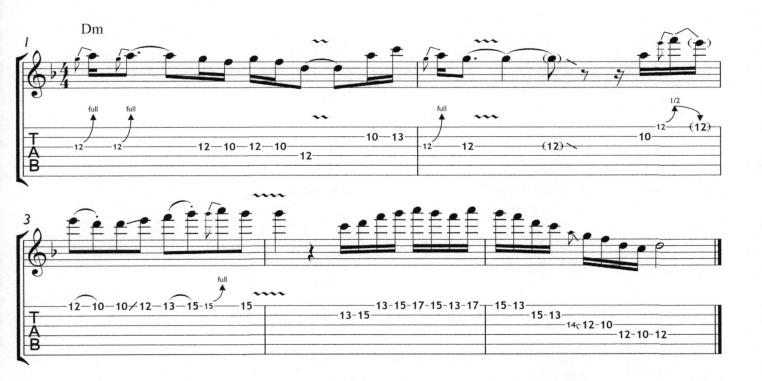

The D Natural Minor scale drives this next melodic phrase. In bar one, to facilitate the jump from the fourth to second string, start the lick with the third finger on the 7th fret of the G string, followed by the second finger on the D string then the third finger on the B string. Bar four features one of Joe's common sextuplet licks, six 1/16th notes played in the space of one beat. This is a real picking challenge so start slowly and work on synchronising the picking and fretting hands with my picking directions.

Example 8b

The next lick is structurally similar to the previous lick, as sparse D minor playing contrasts with an explosive Eric Johnson inspired descending sextuplet run in bar three.

Example 8c

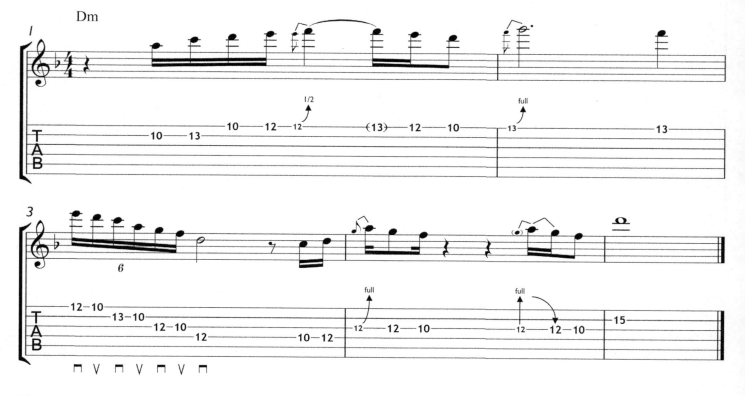

Joe's approach is not all about blistering technique of course and his huge Les Paul driven tone means that sustained bends often conrast the speed.

Example 8d

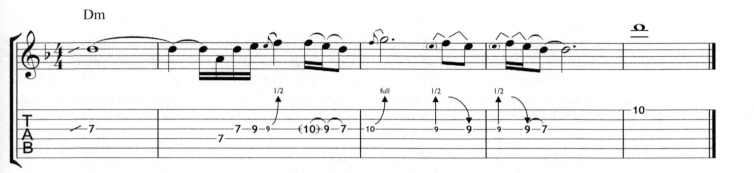

There are many things you can take from Joe's style, but I always come back to his clean, precise picking. Bending from the second (E) to the minor third (F) is a particularly emotive idea over a minor chord but your half step bend from the 5th fret must be pitched perfectly.

Example 8e

Chapter Nine: Buddy Guy

Grammy Award winning bluesman Buddy Guy is a legend within the genre. Influenced by artists like T-Bone Walker, B.B. King and Lightin' Hopkins, he himself has gone on to shape the sound of many younger blues players. Eric Clapton was an early champion and it's testament to Guy's sound and approach that he has often shared major stages with Slowhand.

Buddy Guy started his long and varied career as a sideman. Moving to Chicago in the late 1950s, he started working with Ike Turner before signing to the famous Chess Records label. The partnership didn't go well, with the label trying to shape him into more of a balladeer and jazz musician, which was at odds with his aggressive lead style that had its real home in the clubs. Consequently, his solo career didn't blossom here and instead the label hired him as a session player.

This was something of a blessing and he certainly developed his blues chops during this time, recording for artists like Muddy Waters, Howlin' Wolf and Sonny Boy Williamson, all pioneers of the electric blues scene. It's wrong to label Buddy Guy as just a Chicago bluesman, however, as his style runs much deeper and includes elements of soul, jazz and sometimes even rock.

The Chicago blues sound veers towards the aggressive side of things, so in Guy's intro licks you'll hear powerful, determined phrases that don't hold back. In addition to blues, there is a definite Rock 'n' Roll sound within his playing, so sometimes things get pretty wild! In terms of vocabulary he is very much steeped in the minor pentatonic sound of the blues, but his aggressive attack, biting tone and distinctive, fast vibrato yield his unique character and are part of what has made him a leading player within the blues world.

His powerful style developed, in part, thanks to his showmanship. He often jumped on the bar or climbed onto the tables in the clubs where he performed. Indeed, anyone who has seen Buddy Guy play live will know about his famous 150 foot lead, which means he can walk freely around the venue entertaining all corners up close and personal.

When playing licks in Buddy Guy's style, it's all about conviction, so dig in with the picking hand and go for that hard, aggressive sound. It's useful to make the connection with Jimi Hendrix here, as Buddy Guy was a big influence on his playing. During the 1960s, Hendrix attended one of Buddy Guy's blues workshops and sheepishly asked if he could record the proceedings with his reel to reel player. In both players you'll hear those driven, fuzzy tones with attitude to match.

With his masterful phrasing and raucous tone, Buddy Guy is a great artist to study for intro inspiration. He has played various guitars over the years but seems most comfortable on a Fender Stratocaster and has his own signature model Fender Strat – the famous Polka Dot model he has been using since 1995. Amps are mostly a Fender Bassman, though he has also used a Marshall JCM 800 – not necessarily an amp you'd associate with a blues guitarist, but an obvious choice when you consider his loud, singing lead tones. Beyond this, his gear is quite sparse with a Tubescreamer, Rotovibe and Wah being the only effects he really employs regularly.

Recommended Listening

I Was Walking Through the Woods

Feels Like Rain

Born to Play Guitar

Sometimes an intro phrase is actually a riff and Guy has recorded many riff-based tracks. Here the A Minor Pentatonic scale is used as a riff building tool. Look out for the string skip at the end of the second bar, where the first finger jumps from the 5th fret on the D string to the 5th fret E string. This is cleaner than a barre which can muddy the notes.

Example 9a

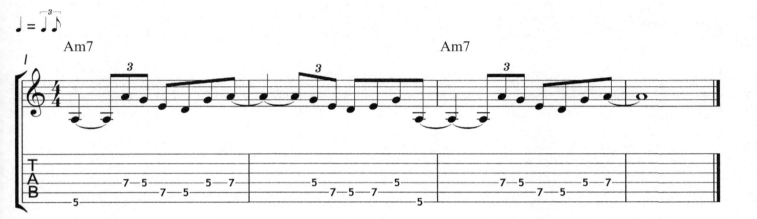

The aggressive, tremelo picked double-stop in bar three is a real Guy-ism. Don't hold back here. Use a fast repeating down/upstroke on the double-stop. Use the third and second fingers to fret the notes and lightly rest the first finger on the strings behind the double-stop to stop the other strings from ringing out.

Example 9b

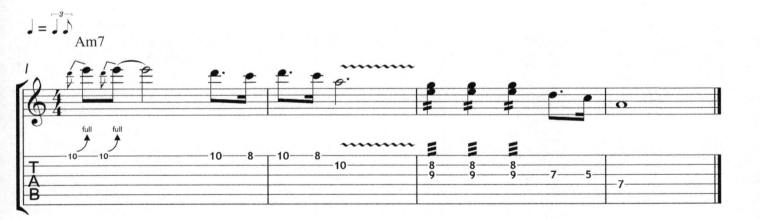

This example is typical of Guy's edgy, almost erratic, approach to blues intros. It's worth experimenting with a fuzzy tone when playing like this, as a clean tone won't give you enough power. The first bend on the E string needs to get up to pitch immediately, but you can contrast this with slower, lazy blues curls in bars three and four.

Example 9c

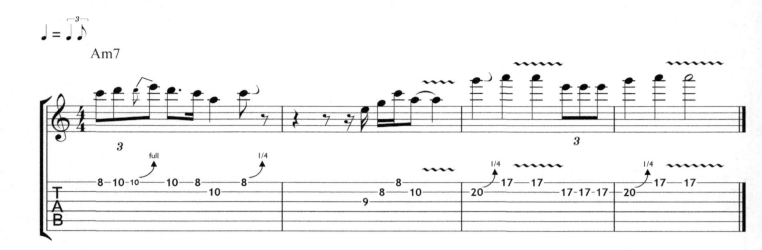

You've worked on Guy's aggressive string bends but at the end of bar one there is the challenge of two 1/32nd notes at the end of beat 4. Don't worry, things aren't going theory mad here, but this rapid fire, off the cuff phrase is common in his style and requires a very fast down/up/down picking pattern. Relax the wrist and go for it following my suggested pick directions.

Example 9d

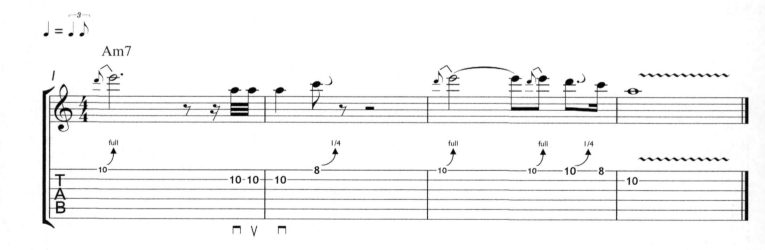

Play the opening of this phrase with just downstrokes for a more aggressive Guy-esque attack. Reinforce the bend in bar two by wrapping the thumb over the neck and use the second or third finger to play the full tone bend on the 7th fret of the G string, followed by the fourth finger for the 8th fret of the B string.

Example 9e

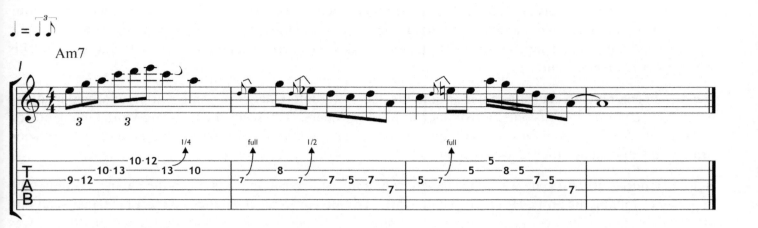

Chapter Ten: Jimi Hendrix

One of the best-known musicians in the history of popular music, Jimi Hendrix is widely credited with having transformed both the sound and playing style of the electric guitar. Born in 1942 in Seattle, USA, as Johnny Allen Hendrix, he later changed his name to James Marshall Hendrix to honour his father James Allen and his late brother Leon Marshall.

Hendrix began playing acoustic guitar around the age of 15 before acquiring an electric guitar and studying the playing styles of famous blues artists such as Muddy Waters, B.B. King and Howling Wolf, among others. Hendrix quickly became infatuated with the instrument and practiced daily for several hours at a time, soon forming his first band called The Velvetones.

Before Hendrix turned 19, he was twice caught riding in a stolen car and was given the choice of doing time in prison or joining the army. He enlisted and, while stationed in Kentucky, requested that his father send him his guitar. His obsession with the instrument led him to often neglect his military duties and in 1962 he was honourably discharged on the grounds of unsuitability.

Upon his discharge, Hendrix began his music career in earnest and started playing in various local bands, eventually working as a sideman with numerous soul and blues musicians, and playing on a well-known circuit of venues in the South. In 1964 he moved to Harlem, New York, and secured a position with the Isley Brothers' back-up band. After a short-lived period with this group he joined the band backing Little Richard and later Curtis Knight. Around this time, the former Animals manager, Chas Chandler, saw Hendrix play in Greenwich Village and brought him to London where he was introduced to drummer Mitch Mitchell and bassist Noel Redding. Together, they formed The Jimi Hendrix Experience.

The Jimi Hendrix Experience quickly began drawing the attention of the music press and also other rock musicians who were stunned by Hendrix's ability and showmanship, which included playing the guitar behind his head and with his teeth.

In the next few years Hendrix released three studio albums to great critical acclaim, with the final album, *Electric Ladyland,* being considered by many as one of the greatest rock albums ever recorded. By this time, Hendrix's songwriting was highly unique and fused perfectly with his legendary guitar skills.

By 1969, Hendrix was reputedly the highest paid rock musician in the world and his set at the Woodstock festival was one of the defining moments of his career, mostly because of his staggering rendition of the US national anthem.

The original Experience trio broke up in June 1969 and Hendrix began to work with bassist Billy Cox and original drummer Mitch Mitchell, before forming the short-lived Band of Gypsys with drummer Buddy Miles. His success continued until 1970, but was sadly increasingly hindered by drug abuse and alcohol-related issues.

On September 18, 1970, Jimi Hendrix died in his sleep from asphyxia while intoxicated with barbiturates. He was just 27 years old.

Hendrix was left-handed and is known for playing a right-handed Fender Stratocaster turned upside down and re-strung. He is associated with the Stratocaster, but also occasionally played other electrics such as the Gibson Flying V and Les Paul. He primarily used Marshall amplifiers live, but in the studio used other makes for different tones. He pioneered the use of many effects devices, including wah-wah pedals, Univibes and fuzz units, along with tape flanging and echo devices, especially on his studio recordings

Recommended Listening

Electric Ladyland

Axis: Bold as Love

Blues

Are You Experienced

Hendrix's blues style is difficult to pin down as he played with such wild abandon. His vocabulary is drawn from the same minor and major pentatonic pool as his peers, but his use of complex, free rhythms, unexpected chromaticism and an effects laden tone make it hard to emulate. Some of these licks will be a challenge and they are on the tamer end of his style! When playing them, try to get in the general ballpark first, then work on matching his rhythms over time. Copying what he did is a great lesson in developing rhythmic control. Check out his various versions of *Red House* to hear what he was capable of in a blues setting.

The following examples are played over a 12/8 groove with a loose, almost psychedelic feel. The progression moves from the I chord (G7) to the IV (C7), so when developing your own intros try using a combination of G minor and major pentatonics and target the chord tones as much as possible. This means aiming for the notes G, B, D and F over the I chord, and C, E, G and Bb when you hit the IV chord.

Example 10a outlines the chords with arpeggios. It's a traditional blues device, similar to how Hendrix played the intro of *Red House*. Consistent rhythm and picking are key here.

Example 10a

The next example features some chromaticism at the end of the lick in bar one, followed by a C minor arpeggio in bar two, which adds tension against the underlying C7 chord. In bars three and four there is a bit more of a frenzied approach, with the rapid bend/release lick at the 13th fret on the B string.

Example 10b

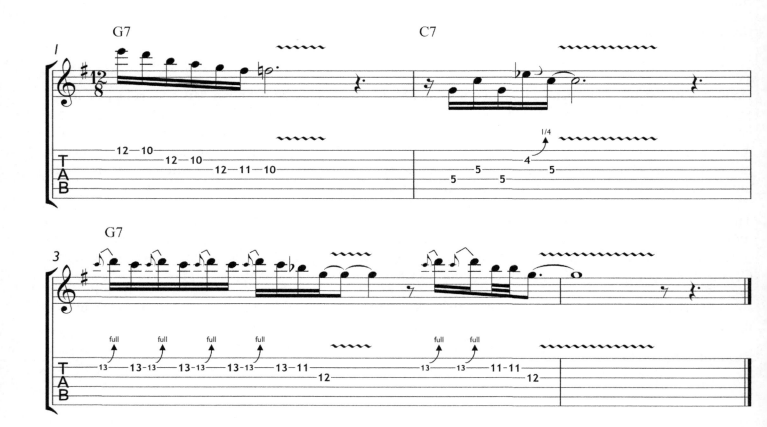

You'll hear country-style bends in Hendrix's blues playing from time to time. To execute the bend at the end of bar one use the third finger to bend the note on the B string at the 18th fret followed by the fourth finger at the 18th fret of the E string. Sustain the bent note against this new note, then re-pick it, so both strings sound simultaneously.

Bar three highlights a typical fast Hendrix-style sequenced lick. Barre the 15th fret with your first finger throughout. After the first pull-off on the high E string, downward pick the B and E strings consistently to get the sequenced loop sounding smooth.

Example 10c

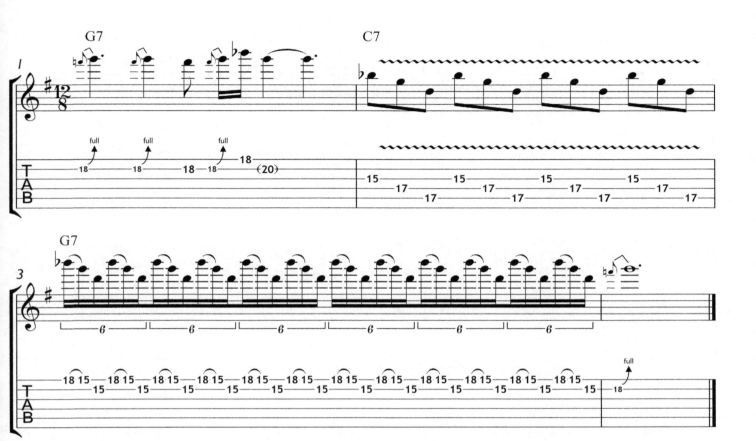

Here, the use of wild rhythms make the G Minor Pentatonic scale sound distinctly Hendrix. The bends at the end of bar three are quite challenging so use the second finger for the bend at the 6th fret of the B string, followed by the third finger on the 7th fret of the G string.

Example 10d

The final Hendrix style example opens with a traditional sounding blues lick in bar one, then gets wilder! Bar two opens with a third finger pre-bend at the 10th fret, followed by notes from a C7 arpeggio (C, Bb, E) and a huge tone and a half bend at the 12th fret of the B string. Remember to add strength and stability to the bend by placing the third finger of the fretting hand at the 12th fret supported by the first and second fingers on the frets behind.

Example 10e

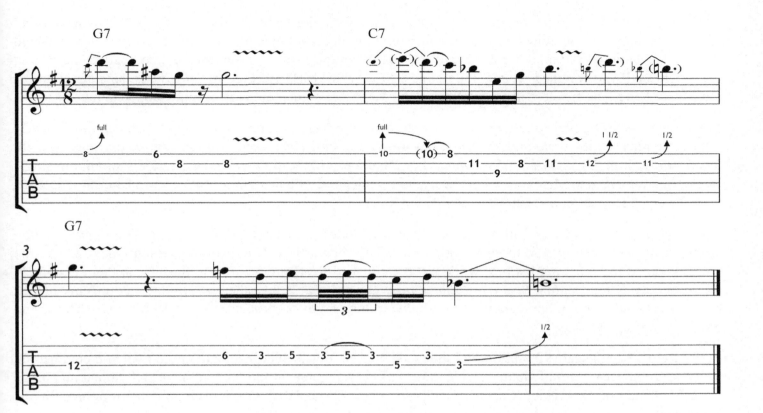

Chapter Eleven: Albert King

Albert King was born Albert Nelson in 1923 on a cotton plantation in Mississippi, USA. He began his musical career by singing Gospel music in church while working in local fields picking cotton. King was nicknamed the "Velvet Bulldozer" due to his sheer size and soulful singing style. He reportedly stood between 6'4" and 6'7" inches tall and weighed around 250 pounds. Along with B.B. and Freddy King, he is considered one of the "Three Kings" of the electric blues, although he was not related to either and simply adopted their surname.

In his early career he played around Arkansas, Indiana and Missouri, before moving to Chicago in the early 1950s. He released his first single in 1953, but it was not until 1963 that he found commercial success with *Don't Throw Your Love On Me So Strong*. After a number of record label changes and disappointing single sales, King relocated to Memphis, where he became associated with the famous Stax record label and recorded with the legendary session group Booker T & the MGs.

King recorded many singles with the group, which included his best-known recording, *Born Under a Bad Sign*, which has been covered by many other blues and rock artists. The recordings King made at this time are considered to be among his best work and the polished R&B productions at Stax made them extremely radio friendly. King's album, *Live Wire/Blues Power* (recorded at Bill Graham's Fillmore Auditorium) helped King gain the attention of many period-blues influenced rock guitarists such as Eric Clapton, Gary Moore and Stevie Ray Vaughan.

In the 1970s, King became increasingly influenced by funk music and, in an attempt to maintain commercial success, produced a series of albums that featured string arrangements and funk influenced rhythm guitar parts. By 1975, King was experiencing contractual issues with the Stax label, which eventually filed for bankruptcy. He moved to another label before taking a four-year hiatus from recording.

King returned to playing the blues in the 1980s, partly due to the renewed interest in the genre created by players like Stevie Ray Vaughan, and despite growing health problems, he continued to tour. He recorded his final studio album in 1984 and continued to perform live right up to his death in 1992 from a heart attack.

King was renowned for having a unique sound and distinctive playing style. His choice of guitar was a Gibson Flying V, and he later had a signature model made. His guitar tone was generally quite clean, although he experimented with mild overdrive to produce a warmer, more vocal sound.

He usually tuned his guitar down from concert pitch and often played in an open tuning, although reports vary on the actual pitches he used. King most commonly used a solid-state acoustic amplifier with twin 15-inch speakers. He rarely used effect pedals but occasionally employed an MXR Phase 90 later in his career.

Distinctively, he used a right-handed guitar but played it upside down in a left-handed position. This meant that the strings were arranged in reverse to a regularly tuned instrument, and this led him to create unique-sounding blues bends that are hard to emulate on a conventionally tuned guitar. King reputedly possessed incredibly strong hands that allowed him to bend strings further in pitch than other players in the idiom.

King's vibrato and string bending approach has been copied by many rock and blues guitarists and it was a major influence on Stevie Ray Vaughan.

Recommended Listening

King of the Blues Guitar

I'll Play the Blues For You

Live Wire/Blues Power

I Wanna Get Funky

Although noted for his string bending prowess, King didn't always play aggressively and frequently used a soft touch with a fairly clean tone. Watching him play one of his extended live blues intros is a masterclass in ebb and flow as he builds his phrases to a crescendo then eases back again. You'll be focusing on the C Minor Pentatonic scale for these examples with a 12/8 feel all the way.

Here King starts by hinting at the V chord (G7) in bar one before moving to a phrase using repetition in bar two. Normally, the fourth finger would be a good choice at the 11th fret, but you may find it easier to execute the quarter tone bend with the third finger. The trill in bar four outlines the classic minor to major third sound (Eb to E) and you should use your first and second fingers for this rapid hammer-on/pull-off motion.

Example 11a

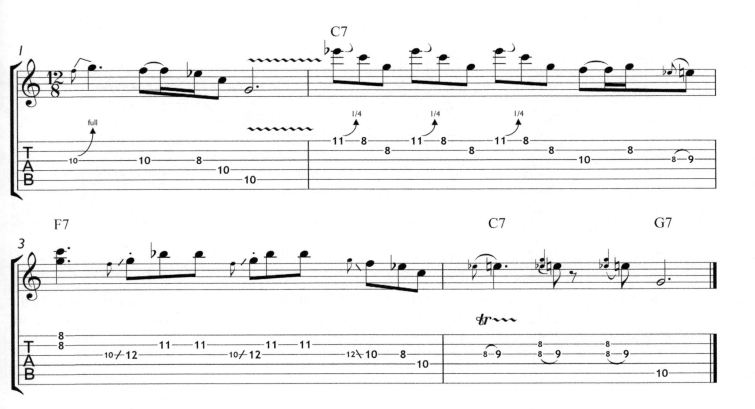

This phrase opens with a classic pick-up lick at the end of bar one – a short, unaccompanied phrase before the band comes in. For this particular move use the first finger barred over both notes at the 8th fret and the third finger for the bend. The last note in bar four looks like a good candidate for fretting with the fourth finger, but for large bends that digit typically doesn't have enough strength, so use a reinforced third finger here.

Example 11b

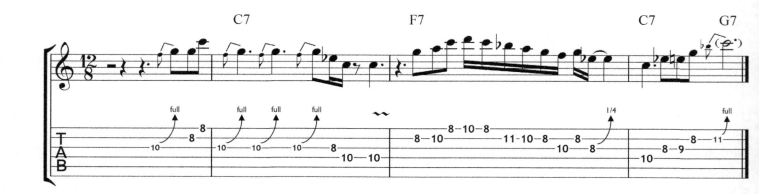

This simple phrase built on C Minor Pentatonic is all about space and simplicity but there are still areas to work on. In bar one, see how it feels to use the third finger or fourth finger for the quarter tone bend. Generally, a four fret span like this suggests the first finger on the lowest note and the fourth on the highest. However, as soon as bends are involved you may find the stronger third finger more suitable. See what works for you (and doesn't hurt!)

Example 11c

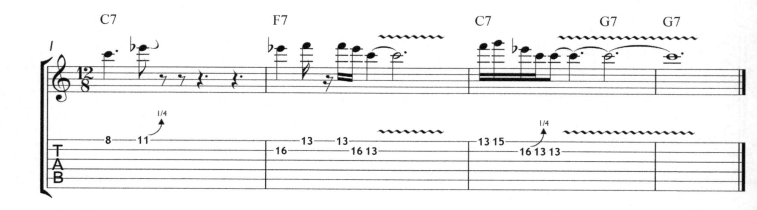

For this next example, it's important to get the all the rhythms in place accurately, so really listen to the recording to hear what's going on. Playing with rhythms that are less predictable and don't fall into simple on/off the beat patterns can help your blues playing sound more authentic.

Example 11d

The lick in bar one is just a little different from what you might expect from the C Minor box shape, as the note on the B string, 8th fret, is so often preceded by the note at the 11th fret. King, however, jumps over to the G string making things sound fresher. A first finger barre over the 8th fret of the E, B and G strings will help here.

Example 11e

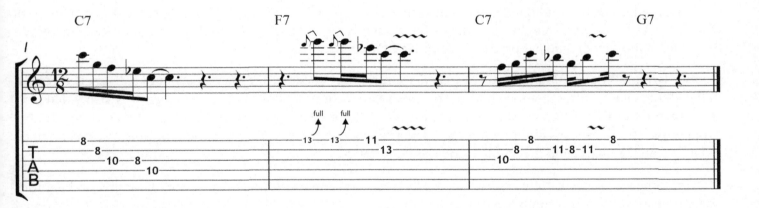

Chapter Twelve: Stevie Ray Vaughan

Stevie Ray Vaughan was born on October 1954 in Dallas, Texas. Initially inspired by his older brother Jimmie's guitar playing, Vaughan received his first instrument at the age of 10, a plastic Sears model. With a natural ear for music and an obsession for blues guitar, Vaughan quickly taught himself to play. By the time he was attending high school he was already performing around the Dallas club circuit.

With few academic aspirations, Vaughan struggled at school, and after a short enrolment on an alternative arts program he soon dropped out of education. He subsequently moved to Austin, Texas, to concentrate on making a living as a musician. Initially earning a steady income was a problem and Vaughan survived by collecting soda and beer bottles for cash while staying at friends' houses. He spent all his spare time playing music, honing his guitar skills and working with the numerous bands that played in the Austin area.

In 1975, Vaughan and other local musicians formed the group Triple Threat. After some line-up changes, the band was renamed Double Trouble, inspired by the Otis Rush song. With Vaughan playing guitar and now singing, the group developed a strong following throughout Texas. By this time, Vaughan's dynamic blues guitar playing was a major attraction for his audiences.

In 1982, Double Trouble caught the attention of Mick Jagger who invited them to play at a party in New York. In the same year, Double Trouble performed at the Montreux Blues & Jazz Festival to a mixed reaction.

While in Switzerland, Vaughan's guitar prowess caught the attention of David Bowie, who asked him to play on his upcoming album, *Let's Dance*. The combination of Vaughan's blues guitar and Bowie's voice proved a commercial success, although despite a lucrative offer to tour with Bowie, Vaughan elected to remain with Double Trouble. Vaughan and his bandmates were quickly signed to Epic Records, where they were mentored by the legendary musician and producer, John Hammond, Sr.

Double Trouble's debut album, *Texas Flood* was surprisingly successful for a blues album and reached No. 38 in the album charts, attracting the attention of rock radio stations across the U.S. Vaughan was also voted Best New Talent and Best Electric Blues Guitarist in the 1983 readers' poll by *Guitar Player* magazine. Double Trouble set off on a successful tour and recorded a second album, *Couldn't Stand the Weather*, which climbed to No. 31 on the charts and eventually turned gold in 1985.

More commercial success followed with recordings and tours that culminated in several Grammy nominations and Vaughan being named both Entertainer of the Year, and Blues Instrumentalist of the Year by The National Blues Foundation in 1985. He was the first white musician to receive both honours.

Despite the musical successes, Vaughan's personal life suffered from his relentless touring and recording schedule. His marriage fell apart and he battled serious drug and alcohol problems. Following a collapse on tour in Europe in 1986, Vaughan checked himself into a rehabilitation centre. He stayed away from the musical spotlight for about a year to recover and in 1988 he and Double Trouble started performing again. In June 1989, the trio released their fourth studio album, *In Step*.

In the spring of 1990, Vaughan and his brother Jimmie began work on an album scheduled for that Fall. *Family Style* was scheduled for October, but sadly Vaughan didn't live to see it.

On August 26, 1990, after a show in Wisconsin, Vaughan left the venue on a helicopter bound for Chicago. Due to heavy fog, the helicopter crashed into a ski hill just after take-off killing everyone on board. Vaughan was buried at Laurel Land Memorial Park in South Dallas and more than 1,500 people attended his memorial service.

Stevie Ray Vaughan's guitar style was heavily influenced by many of the blues and rock greats, most notably Albert King and Jimi Hendrix. Vaughan had a strong left-hand vibrato and great skill with string bending. Primarily favouring minor and major pentatonics and the blues scales, he also displayed a sophisticated knowledge of jazz chord voicings.

Vaughan was closely associated with the Fender Stratocaster guitar and owned many of them throughout his career, his favourite being a 1959 model he named Number One. He strung his guitars with extremely heavy-gauge strings and tuned down a half-step to facilitate easier string bending.

He generally favoured tube amplifiers such as the Fender Super Reverb and Vibrolux, although at times he recorded with Marshall and Dumble amplifiers too. For effects, he used an early model Ibanez Tube Screamer and a Wah Wah pedal, but did also experiment with other effects such as Leslie speakers.

Recommended Listening

Texas Flood

Couldn't Stand the Weather

The Sky Is Crying

SRV

These intro licks will explore how Stevie would open a fast tempo blues/rock riff-based track.

Stevie Ray Vaughan had no problem starting faster songs and combining hammer-ons and pull-offs with alternate picking can help. Play the D Blues scale phrase on beat 3 in bar four with a smooth pull-off, starting with the second finger at the 12th fret followed by the third finger, leading back to the first finger at the 10th fret.

Example 12a

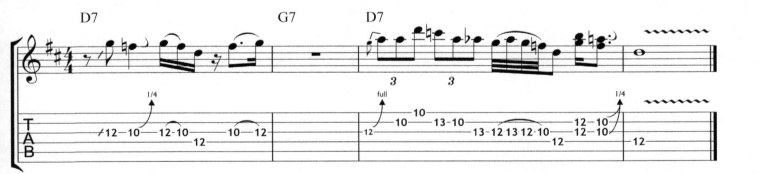

The double-stops fill things out in Example 12b, particularly in bar three, in this high-energy lick. You can use whichever combination of fingers feel natural to you for the double-stops, but I use my second and third fingers. Remember to mute the B string for the octaves passage in bar five.

Example 12b

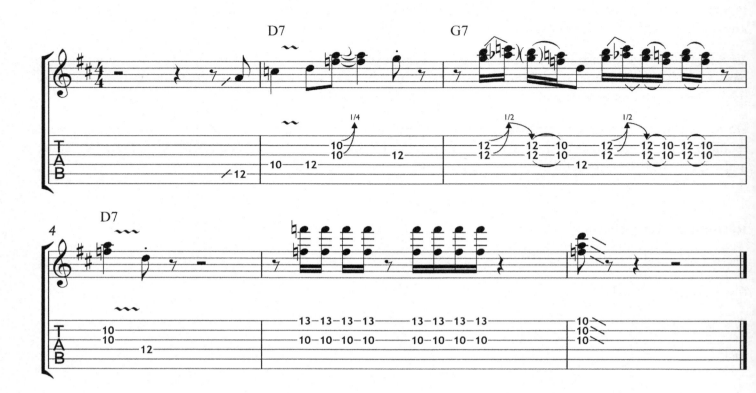

SRV's double-stop bends were most likely influenced by Albert King and it's a great sounding technique. When playing the phrase in bar four, use the same fingering choice as the previous exercise. The double-stops in bar four are rapid and need to be strummed rather than picked. Use your third finger to play the 14th fret with the second finger on the 13th fret. This leaves the first finger free to sit on the strings behind these notes, giving a nice percussive attack as you hit the surrounding muted strings with wild abandon!

Example 12c

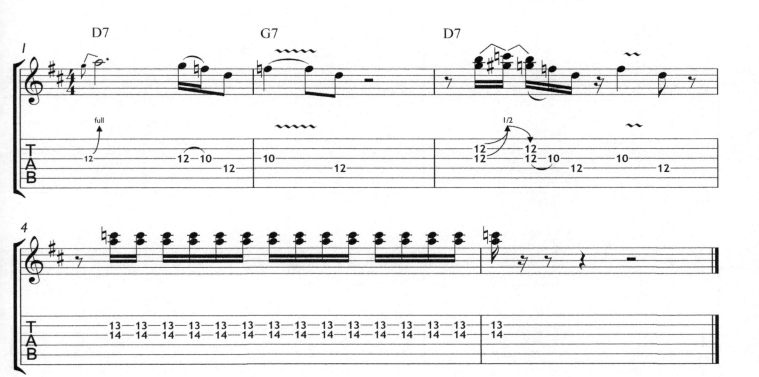

Start the next intro with the third finger at the 15th fret and use a fast/wide vibrato to match the up-tempo feel of the track, maintaining this approach when you reach the end of bar two. Bar four's SRV style double-stops feature melodic movement rather than bends. Use a first finger barre for the double-stop at the 10th fret and the third and fourth fingers for the next one.

Example 12d

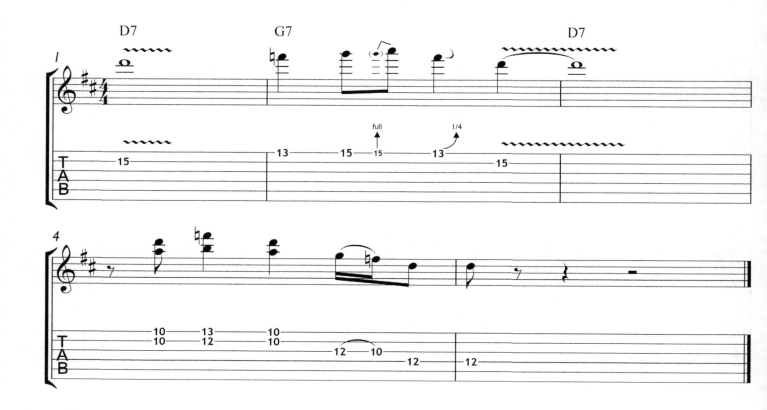

The final SRV phrase has a "call and response" feel to it and is achieved by starting high in the D Minor Pentatonic box shape then going lower in the same box. The phrase in bar one is a classic lick you probably know, but at this speed remember to use the first finger to barre both the E and B strings at the 10th fret.

Example 12e

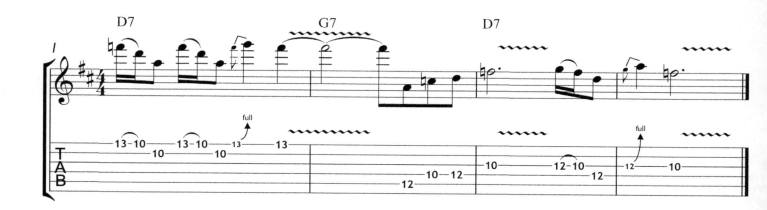

Chapter Thirteen: Elmore James

One of the most influential slide guitarists and blues songwriters of the 20th Century, Elmore James was born Elmore Brooks in 1918 in Richland, Mississippi, USA. He became a significant influence upon many subsequent blues and rock artists, several of whom covered his material. James' slide guitar style influenced many players after his death, and he was a particular favourite of Jimi Hendrix, Roy Buchanan, Duane Allman, and Brian Jones of the Rolling Stones.

Raised as the illegitimate son of a 15-year-old field hand called Leola Brooks, his father was most likely a man called Joe Willie "Frost" James, and Elmore adopted his surname. He began making music around the age of 12, using a rudimentary one-stringed instrument called a diddley bow (or jitterbug). While still a teenager, he regularly performed at local dances under the stage names of Joe Willie James and Cleanhead.

During World War II, James joined the United States Navy, was promoted to coxswain and took part in the invasion of Guam during the Pacific campaign. Upon his discharge, he returned to central Mississippi and settled in the town of Canton with his adopted brother, Robert Holston.

Working in Holston's electrical shop, he created his unique electric guitar sound using spare parts from the shop and an unusual placement of two DeArmond pickups. Around this time James also learned that he had a serious heart condition which would affect much of his later life.

James' writing and playing were heavily influenced by early blues masters such as Robert Johnson, Tampa Red and Kokomo Arnold, and he later recorded several of Red's compositions.

Elmore James began recording for the Trumpet Records label in January 1951, starting out as a sideman for Sonny Boy Williamson and Willie Love. He made his recording debut as a session leader in August of 1951 with his best-known song *Dust My Broom* (originally composed by Robert Johnson). This track became an unexpected chart success in 1952.

James left his contract with Trumpet Records a short time later to sign with the Bihari Brothers, a move that was engineered by their talent scout Ike Turner, who played guitar and piano on some of his recordings.

During the mid-1950s, James recorded for a variety of other record labels including Flair Records, Modern Records and Meteor Records. Additionally, he played lead guitar on the 1954 hit, *TV Mama*.

By 1959, James was recording for Fire Records and released some of his best-known work including *The Sky Is Crying* and *Shake Your Moneymaker*. These songs later became favourite covers for artists such as Fleetwood Mac and Stevie Ray Vaughan.

Elmore James passed away from a heart attack in May 1963 at the age of 45, while preparing for a European tour.

James' choice of guitars and amplification was remarkably simple, usually favouring a Kay acoustic guitar fitted with a DeArmond pickup over the sound hole or sometimes a Silvertone solid body guitar. For amplification, he is reported to have used an early model Gibson combo. Like many slide guitarists, James favoured the use of open tunings.

He played frequently using the open D tuning (as on *Dust My Broom*) which is D A D F# A D (tuned from low to high).

Recommended Listening

Blues After Hours

Dust My Broom

The Sky is Crying

King of the Slide Guitar

You can emulate the sound of a slide player to some extent by sliding into phrases and using a wide, fast vibrato with the fretting hand, and that's what we'll do here. In essence, this means shaking the notes as much as possible, especially when playing double-stops. Apply a lot more vibrato than you would normally. Listen to Elmore James and you'll hear how much he is using the slide to shake the notes.

This first Elmore James intro lick features his double-stops and triplets approach and is similar to the T-Bone Walker phrase you studied earlier. The rhythm is very distinctive, so to get this sounding right remember to slide into the double-stop at the start of each beat.

Example 13a

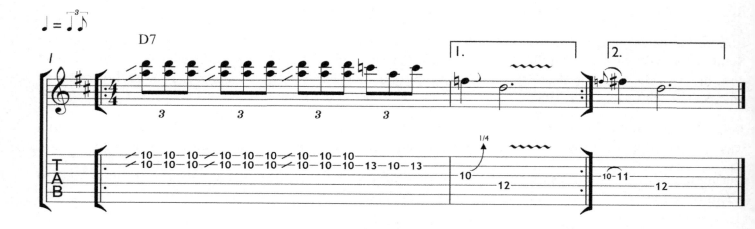

Here is the type of Elmore James phrase that found its way into Clapton's playing, amongst others. It's D Minor Pentatonic all the way, with the first finger starting at the 10th fret. A useful tip is to pull this finger down towards the ground when doing quarter tone bends. Going with gravity is easier than fighting it when it comes to the small blues curl!

Example 13b

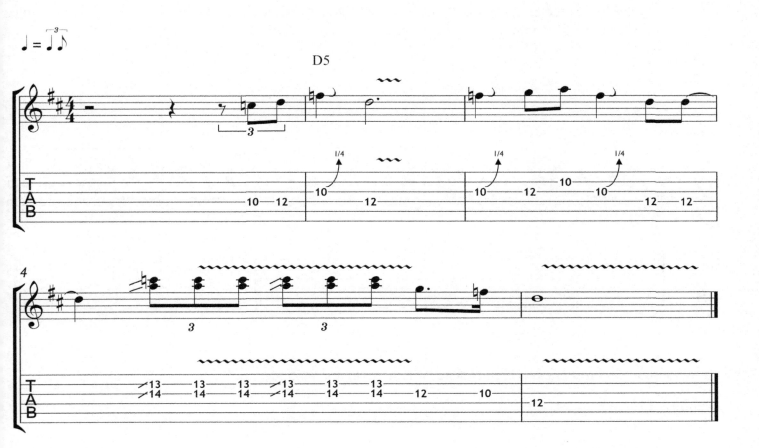

The third Elmore James lick mimics slide playing again, but this time you are playing each note in the double-stop individually. Barre the first finger at the 10th fret and shake the whole hand to produce an extreme vibrato. Be careful not to release the pressure on the first finger though, as you'll dampen the notes. A relaxed wrist will help you focus on keeping that first finger in place.

Example 13c

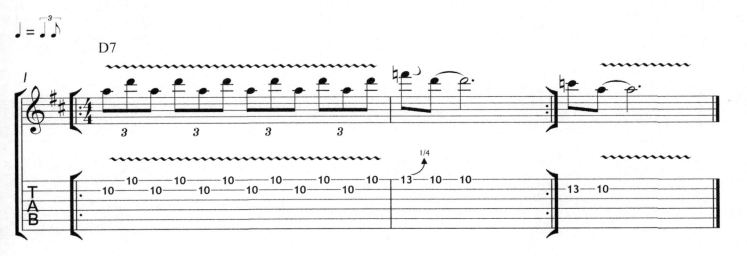

The next example features a quite simple phrase with plenty of space, but there is a fingering consideration at the end of bar one/start of bar two. Use the third finger at the 10th fret of the B string followed by the first finger at the 8th fret of the E. The temptation is to then move the third finger to the 10th fret of the G string, but you'll find that the second finger will give you a smoother overall sound.

Example 13d

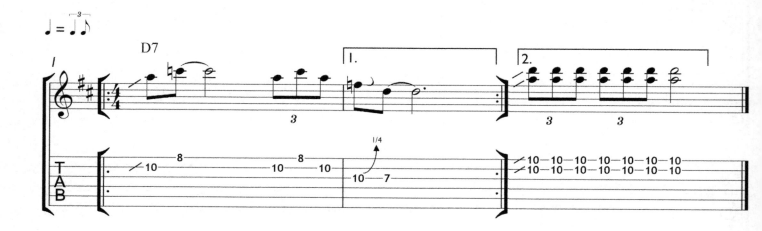

Here's a final Elmore James style intro featuring more double-stop ideas.

Example 13e

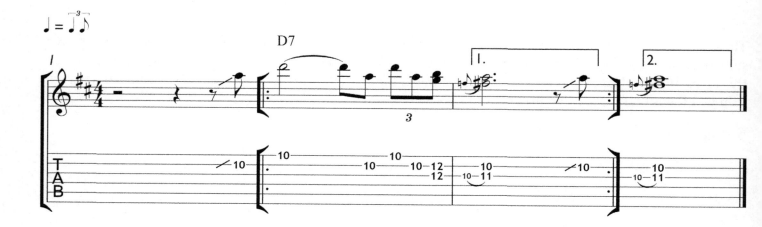

Chapter Fourteen: Larry Carlton

Larry Eugene Carlton was born in March, 1948, in Torrance, California. He began studying guitar at the age of 6 and soon became interested in jazz through listening to legendary guitar players such as Joe Pass, Barney Kessel and Wes Montgomery. He was also attracted to the blues guitar playing of B.B. King. He attended junior college and Long Beach State College while playing professionally at clubs in and around the Los Angeles area.

Carlton's rapidly developing playing expertise and background in both jazz and rock/pop music made him a rising star within the Los Angeles session scene of the 1970s. Eventually playing on hundreds of recording sessions and movie soundtracks, he was equally at home with pop, jazz, rock and even country record dates, making him a highly sought after studio guitarist. His work with Steely Dan and Joni Mitchell drew much critical praise and his legendary solo on *Kid Charlemagne* by Steely Dan is considered one of the finest recorded guitar solos of all time, as ranked by *Rolling Stone* magazine. He worked with virtually every major record producer from the 1970s and 80s and his musical versatility saw him appear on over 100 gold records.

Alongside his session work, Carlton has also had a long running solo career beginning with his 1968 debut album *With A Little Help From My Friends*. In the mid-70s he built a home studio and called it Room 335 after the Gibson ES-335 model guitar he'd played for many years as his main instrument. He has recorded most of his albums at Room 335 and one of his best-known compositions is named after the studio. Carlton produced six solo albums from 1978 to 1984 and had some notable commercial success with his version of Santo Farina's track *Sleepwalk*. He was also a member of the jazz fusion group The Crusaders and in 1981 he received a Grammy Award for Best Pop Instrumental Performance for the theme from the popular U.S. TV series *Hill Street Blues*. Carlton also produced a live album called *Last Nite* in 1986.

In 1988, with his solo career progressing strongly, he was shot in the throat by a teenager outside the Room 335 studio and suffered nerve and vocal cord damage, which delayed the completion of the album he was working on at the time, *On Solid Ground*. His left arm was paralyzed and for six months he was unable to play properly. Thankfully, he recovered after this incident and has gone on to record more solo albums and has worked with the group *Fourplay* amongst others.

In more recent years, Carlton has collaborated with fellow studio guitarists Lee Ritenour and Steve Lukather, and he was also commissioned to compose music for the king of Thailand, Bhumibol Adulyadej, in honour of the king's birthday. Carltons' other musical awards include a Grammy Award for Best Pop Instrumental Performance for *Minute by Minute* in 1987, and further Grammy Awards for Best Pop Instrumental Album, *No Substitutions: Live in Osaka* in 2001 and Best Pop Instrumental Album, *Take Your Pick* in 2010.

Carlton's highly distinctive playing style mixes bebop jazz lines with an almost pedal-steel like string bending approach. His use of mixed triads in his solos contrasts with many of the more scale-orientated players of his generation. An inventive, melodic and highly expressive soloist, many artists have taken advantage of his distinct playing style to complement their music.

Carlton is probably best known for the use of his 1969 Gibson ES-335 guitar. In fact, he gained the nickname "Mr 335" for playing this particular instrument, which became a mainstay of the LA studio guitar scene in the 1970-80s. Other guitars he has owned and played include a 1951 Fender Telecaster, a 1964 Fender Stratocaster, and a 1955 Gibson Les Paul Special.

For amplifiers he has used a Fender Vibrolux and Princeton, but his standard setup generally includes a Dumble amplifier, made by legendary amp designer Howard Dumble. Carlton uses effects sparingly in his playing, but does employ some delay and reverb on his signature guitar sound.

Recommended Listening

Larry Carlton

Last Nite

The Royal Scam – Steely Dan

The following intros use a heavy swing feel and go beyond the usual minor pentatonic cliches to include arpeggios that outline the sound of the chord progression. If you are playing this sort of stuff in a live scenario, it's well worth spending some time studying the aforementioned jazz players and their arpeggio-based approach, as it's easy for the inexperienced player to get lost when they stray from familiar pentatonic box shapes.

You'll also hear the use of chromatic passing notes i.e. notes that don't belong to the key signature. Typically, these are used to add a moment of dissonance, a hallmark of jazz. If used carefully they are a great way to emphasise the tension and release aspect of good blues playing.

Before playing through these examples take a look at the chord progression and you'll see that while it's essentially a blues I to V sequence in the key of G (G7 to C7), there is also a ii-V-I progression at the end (Am7 – D7 – G7) which is drawn from the jazz world. Players like Carlton aim to hit chord tones and "outside" notes when playing, so that they are really playing the changes and thinking about each note choice.

Carlton is adept at combining ideas to effortlessly outline the chord progression and this first example begins by moving between G minor and major pentatonic scales, always focusing on the chord tones. Bars three and five takes a Carlton-esque approach to really home in on the G7 chord tones.

Example 14a

Example 14b goes uses a G major arpeggio in bar two to outline the sound of the chord. Bar three's lick outlines the C7 chord with a brief foray into the C Mixolydian scale (C, D, E, F, G, A, Bb) before moving back into a G Major Pentatonic phrase in bar four, spiced up with some chromatic notes. There are more chromatic passing notes over the ii-V progression before a lick that combines G minor and major pentatonic scales in the final bar.

Example 14b

Example 14c begins by mixing G major and minor pentatonics to create a phrase that lands on the b7 (Bb) of the IV chord (C7). Chromaticism is used over the Am7 and D7 chords before resolving to the G root note in the final bar. This shows how Larry often develops motif ideas in his phrasing. Start bar four with the second finger at the 4th fret followed by the third finger. Quickly move the third finger to the 5th fret of the G string and follow this with the first, then second fingers.

65

Example 14c

Here's a slippery idea that glides between G major and minor pentatonics with chromaticism. This is followed by a typical Carlton repeating motif based using the G Blues scale (G, Bb, C, D, F) over the rest of the chord sequence, but notice how the triplet rhythm adds character, allowing the lick to be repeated without becoming stale. From bar three, adhere to the one-finger-per-fret rule to play this.

Example 14d

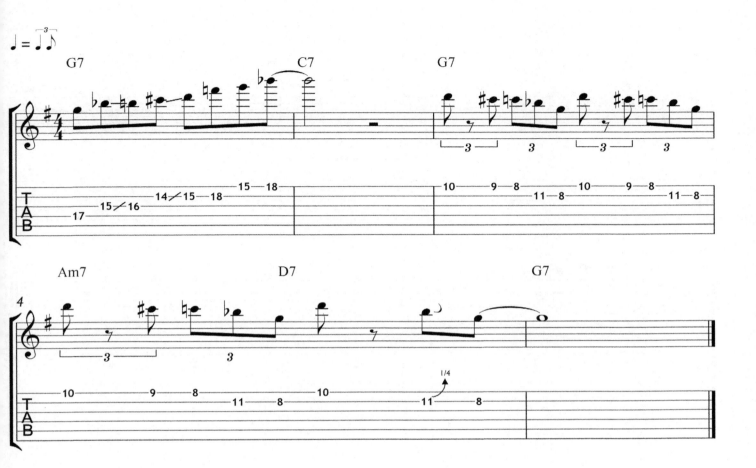

The last phrase starts with a sparse G Minor Pentatonic idea over the I and IV chords before a jazz-inflected triplet laden phrase. Try using my fingering suggestions (at the right of each note head). Over the Am7 chord, the line hints at A Dorian, while a superimposed G major arpeggio moving to a G Blues scale lick are played on the D7. Bars 3-4 have some fingering challenges so I've written suggested finger numbers by the noteheads.

Example 14e

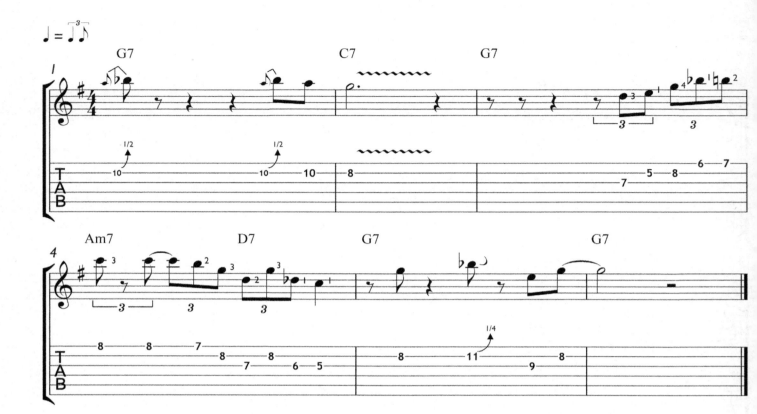

Chapter Fifteen: Robben Ford

Robben Ford was born in Woodlake, California, in 1951 and taught himself to play guitar at around 14 years old, having first played the saxophone. His first influence on guitar was the legendary American blues guitarist Mike Bloomfield, although he later expanded his listening to jazz. Ford is a diverse guitarist with strong blues roots that underpin most of his music

At age 18, Ford moved to San Francisco to form the Charles Ford Band (named after his father who was also a guitarist), and the group was hired to play with Charlie Musselwhite for nine months in 1972. They recorded two albums, *The Charles Ford Band* and *Discovering the Blues*, and Ford also recorded the albums *Live* and *Spoonful* with Jimmy Witherspoon.

Later in the '70s, Ford changed musical direction and became a member of the jazz-fusion group The L.A. Express with saxophonist Tom Scott. This group lasted until 1976, collaborated with Joni Mitchell on two albums, and supported George Harrison on his 1974 American tour. After leaving the L.A. Express, Ford recorded his first solo album, *The Inside Story*. He used West Coast studio musicians who would eventually form the fusion group The Yellowjackets in 1977. Ford played with them until 1983, while also building his solo career and doing session work.

In 1986, Ford toured with trumpeter Miles Davis and spent two separate periods (1985 and 1987) playing with Japanese saxophonist Sadao Watanabe. Much of Ford's work around this period was in the jazz-fusion genre until the release of *Talk To Your Daughter* in 1988. The album was a noticeable return to Ford's blues roots and included a stirring cover of *Born Under A Bad Sign*.

In the early '90s, Ford formed The Blue Line and recorded two of the finest blues-rock albums of his career: *Robben Ford and the Blue Line* and *Tiger Walk*.

In 1999, he released the album *Sunrise* on Rhino and later *Supernatural* on the Blue Thumb label. In 2002 Ford signed to the Concord Jazz label and released *Blue Moon*, followed by *Keep on Running* (2003) and *Truth* (2007).

Ford was a special guest on Larry Carlton's *Live in Tokyo* album, which he followed with the *Soul on Ten* live album in 2009. In 2013, Ford began his label association with Provogue and released the studio album *Bringing It Back Home* which comprised mostly blues and RnB covers played by an all-star band. Later, he recorded an album with a group of A-list session musicians in a single day at Nashville's Sound Kitchen studio. *A Day in Nashville* was released in February 2014.

Robben Ford has received five Grammy Award nominations and was named one of the 100 Greatest Guitarists of the 20th Century by *Musician* magazine.

Robben is a diverse musician who draws from many different genres in his playing. His sublime blues phrasing is probably the most prominent feature of his playing, but he also draws upon a considerable knowledge of jazz harmony and different chord scales. He regularly employs symmetrical scales and extended arpeggios along with more typical pentatonic and blues scale lines.

His equipment setup is usually a Gibson Les Paul or Fender Telecaster played through a tube amplifier (usually Fender, Marshall or his much-favoured Dumble). Ford also uses some digital delay and reverb but rarely to excess, instead preferring a fairly pure clean or overdriven guitar tone.

Robben Ford and the Blue Line

Handful of Blues

Talk To Your Daughter

A Day in Nashville

This example shows how Ford might typically highlight chord tones with an arpeggio in bar one, then introduce chromaticism in bar two while weaving in and out of the minor and major pentatonic scales. Bar five's tense phrase combines the major 6th (in this case A) with a minor third (Eb). There's a great deal going on here so I've included fretting hand fingerings by the noteheads to help you work your way through.

Example 15a

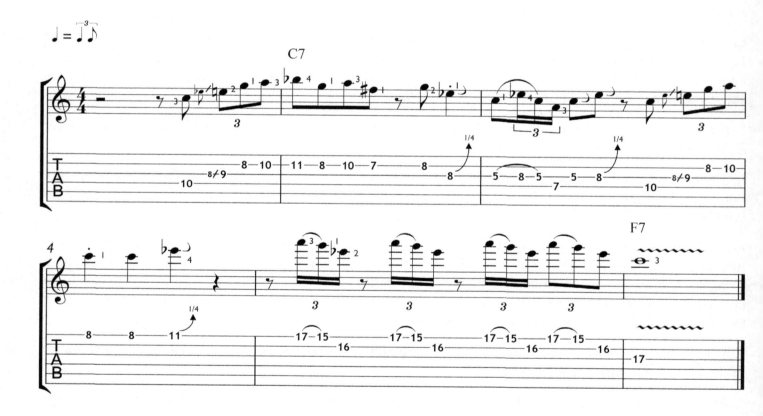

The next intro lick is mostly derived from the C Minor Pentatonic scale but Ford's delicious phrasing really brings it to life with quarter tone bends and triplet rhythms. The move to the IV chord, F7, is anticipated by playing an F7 arpeggio at the end of bar four.

Example 15b

Example 15c is all about restraint. A fragment of a C major arpeggio is used to outline the chord in the first bar. Like any idea, arpeggios can become formulaic and predictable, but in Ford's hands he spices them up with interesting rhythms and space. Bar three brings in the C Blues scale and a cool double-stop phrase. The intro finishes by outlining an F9 arpeggio (F, A, C, E, G) over the F7 chord.

Example 15c

Breaking away from the predictable patterns within the minor pentatonic box can yield some great, modern sounding ideas. Here, the triplet rhythms of the descending lick in bar one are applied to a line based on 4th intervals to create a truly modern blues sound. Also check out the modern sounding lick using ascending 4ths over the F7 chord.

Example 15d

Robben will also take a more traditional approach at times, such as in this last example. Using chord fragments in intro phrases and solos is a great tool to thicken up the sound and reinforce the harmony (check out the C9 and F9 chords in the last two bars). In bar two, use the third finger to barre across the 10th fret of the D, G and B strings to create a triplestop. Follow this with an index finger double-stop barre at the 8th fret.

Example 15e

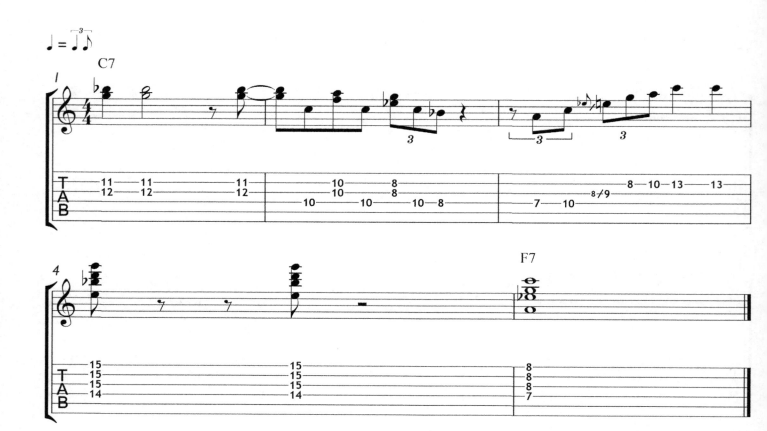

Chapter Sixteen: Robert Cray

As much a songwriter as a guitar player, Robert Cray's soulful take on the blues has led to him win five Grammys and tour the globe as a headline act or in support to blues superstars like Eric Clapton. Influenced by Albert Collins, Freddie King and Muddy Waters, Cray started the first iteration of The Robert Cray Band in the late 1970s. He was embraced by the blues world and over the following decade he recorded with Albert Collins and John Lee Hooker among others.

Born in Columbus, Georgia, in 1953, he took up guitar while in High School. By age twenty he had formed his own band and was touring the West Coast regularly, working for a time in Albert Collin's backing band. He released his first album, *Who's Been Talkin'* in 1980 and had moderate success with his next two albums, *Bad Influence* and *False Accusations*.

Cray's 1985 release *Showdown!* featured Albert Collins and the following year he released *Strong Persuader* which cemented his position as a blues A-lister. He later recorded and performed alongside artists like John Lee Hooker, Eric Clapton and Stevie Ray Vaughan.

The blues scene in America was quite stagnant in the 1980s and artists like Cray and Stevie Ray Vaughan gave it a much needed shot in the arm with their brand of exciting, song-driven blues. Both had a reverence for their heroes, while looking forward. As Keith Richards remarked, "[Robert Cray] has one foot in the past and one foot in the future."

Unlike the work of some blues artists, the tracks on *Strong Persuader* were solid songs, not just vehicles for lengthy guitar solos, and arguably fit more in the RnB genre than straight blues. Cray's tone is also highly discinctive and he wears his Albert Collins influence on his sleeve. His bright, punchy, sometimes cutting licks and solos catch the ear immediately. His lines are generally quite staccatto and don't feature the long, sustained notes of Joe Bonamassa or Gary Moore.

This makes Cray an interesting artist to study for intros. His style forces us to think about how to structure the flow of ideas and the use of space between phrases. Sometimes a ton of space can be a good thing, as it sets up tension without us having to play anything.

Being a songwriter, Robert Cray's intro licks usually serve the purpose of setting up the rest of the song. He's not unlike Clapton in this regard and functions like a good producer, knowing when restraint is better than overblown licks. This is a great lesson to learn - we don't want to peak on the intro and then have the mood go down from there! In the following intro licks you will see how Cray uses minor pentatonic approaches in a restrained and melodic context that sound cohesive and well thought out.

Cray's crisp, cutting guitar tone is a useful reference for how to get a guitar intro to really push through in a full band mix. He has been a Fender Stratocaster player for most of his career and has a signature model which deviates from classic Strat design in that it has a hardtail bridge rather than a floating tremelo. He has used a number of amps, from Fender Twins and Bassmans, but these days relies on a pair of Matchless Clubman amps.

Recommended Listening

Showdown!

Strong Persuader

Nothin But Love

Using the D Minor Pentatonic scale throughout Example 16a, here is a catchy Cray-style motif that ends with a final flurry of notes in bar four then a sustained note in bar five. Play this with authority to get that Cray sound in place! Grace notes feature often in his playing (notes that are sounded but only very briefly). The first example of this is halfway through bar one, where the third finger must strike the note at the 12th fret before sliding immediately up to the 14th fret.

Example 16a

One of the great things about blues is how most of the players draw from the same source – the minor pentatonic scale – but through note choice, phrasing and rhythm still sound like themselves. Cray's biting, spiky style is on display here using the D Minor Pentatonic box.

Example 16b

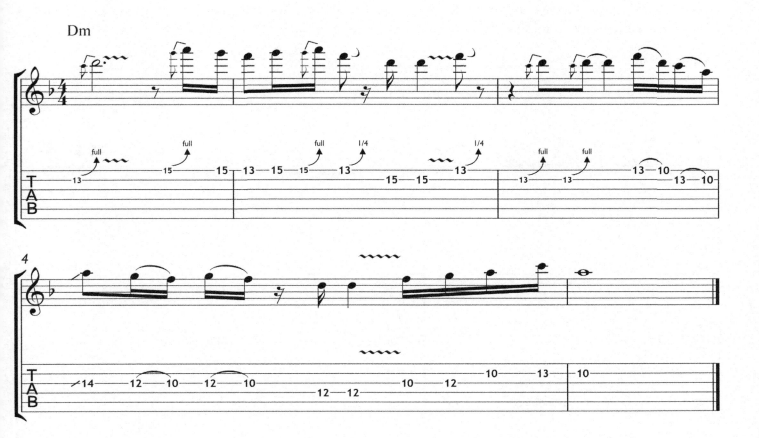

Cray often creates lines that, though they sound quite busy, remain cohesive thanks to repetition and consistency in the rhythms and note choice. Here flurries of notes are followed by restrained, sustained ideas. Don't outstay your welcome or step on the toes of the rest of the band! This is a good exercise for the picking hand as every note is picked. Make sure you use consistent down/up alternate picking throughout.

Example 16c

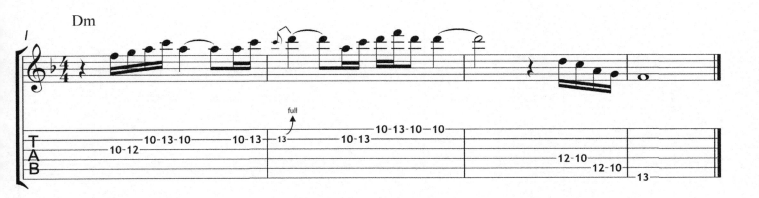

The next example shows the power of correctly resolving licks. Bar one starts with a long stream of notes using D Minor Pentatonic before resolving to the D root note on the D string, 12th fret. This approach is repeated at the end of bar two, but this time the line resolves to the 5th of the key (A) on the B string, 10th fret. Finally, there are more "tumbling" notes before a resolution to the root to set the song up.

Example 16d

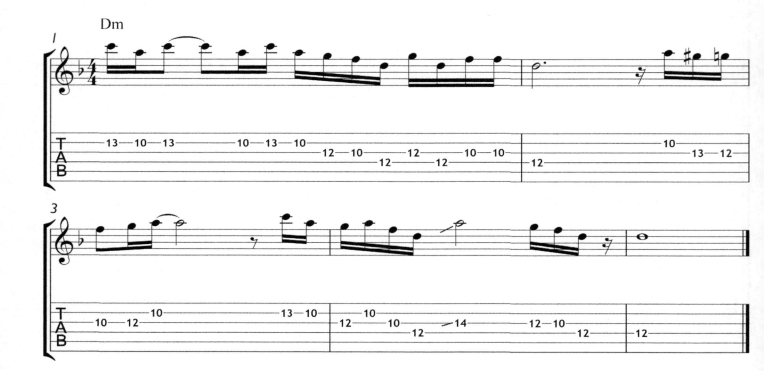

We've seen before that restricting a line to just two strings, as in this example, can create an intro that is restrained and melodic. Rhythm and note choice keep things interesting and it doesn't feel like this intro needs to say anything else before the song begins.

Example 16e

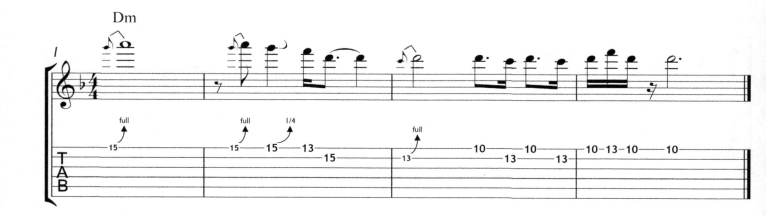

Chapter Seventeen: Gary Moore

Robert William Gary Moore was born in 1952 in Belfast, Northern Ireland, and began learning the guitar at the age of 8 with an old acoustic instrument. Despite being left-handed, he learned to play right-handed and studied by listening to his favourite recordings. He left Belfast and moved to Dublin when he was just 16 years old, determined to pursue a career as a professional musician.

Heavily influenced by Peter Green, Jimi Hendrix, Albert King, Buddy Guy and Eric Clapton, Moore quickly developed a unique blues-rock style that would remain with him throughout his career. In Dublin, he joined the group Skid Row and began a long association with bassist and songwriter Phil Lynott (of Thin Lizzy).

In 1970, he left Ireland to move to London and began working with his own group, The Gary Moore Band, who released their debut album *Grinding Stone* in 1973. By 1974, Moore was working again with Phil Lynott in Thin Lizzy as the replacement for Eric Bell, and this began a long association for Moore with the group. From 1975 to 1978 Moore played with the group Colosseum II before working again with Thin Lizzy, this time replacing Brain Robertson.

After finally leaving Thin Lizzy in 1979, Moore embarked on a successful solo career. With the continued support of Phil Lynott, he produced one of his most memorable songs in *Parisienne Walkways*. During the 1980s, Moore was mostly producing hard rock albums, where his fiery, dynamic guitar style featured heavily. He changed musical direction significantly in 1990 to produce a series of successful blues albums beginning with *Still Got The Blues* (1990), and collaborated with many well-known blues artists. He later returned to mainstream rock, but again moved back to more blues-based material in 2001.

Moore was still actively recording and performing when he tragically passed away from a heart attack in 2011 at the age of 58. He is one of finest blues/rock guitarists to have lived and his playing style and musicality are benchmarks for any contemporary player.

Gary Moore possessed formidable technique on the instrument and was capable of high-speed picking and legato passages. Drawing from pentatonic, blues and modal scales, he was equally adept at rock, blues, fusion, and even some jazz guitar styles. Like many players from a blues background, Moore had a highly developed left-hand vibrato and was particularly skilled in string bending. He employed many techniques that are now commonplace in rock guitar, such as tapping, sweep picking and fast legato sequences.

Most commonly associated with the Gibson Les Paul guitar, Moore also played a Fender Stratocaster at several points in his career (and also some Ibanez guitars), but it is the Les Paul that has endured as his principal instrument. He used a 1959 Les Paul Standard (bought from Peter Green), famous for its distinctive out-of-phase pickup configuration. This guitar featured on many of Moore's (and Green's) most well-known recordings. Taking advantage of the Gibson's natural qualities, he was able to create a rich, sustaining tone which became something of a trademark for him.

Long associated with Marshall amplifiers, Gary Moore's sound was raw and heavily overdriven, yet retained great clarity even at high volume. He played through both combo amplifiers and stack configurations, preferring the latter for live work.

Although Moore used small pedalboards, his sound was generally devoid of obvious effects processing, except for the occasional use of delay and wah-wah. The majority of his signature tones were produced from his guitars and amplifier.

Recommended Listening

Still Got The Blues

Blues For Greeny

Blues Alive

After Hours

This first example breaks away from pentatonic ideas and uses the A Natural Minor scale (A, B, C, D, E, F, G) with a brief foray into A Harmonic Minor via the G# note in bar six (B string, 9th fret). The result blends the melodic approach of rock with the phrasing and sustain of the blues. Start off by playing the B string at the 15th fret with the third finger, bend the note and sustain it, then use the fourth finger to play the 15th fret of the E string so that both notes ring together.

Example 17a

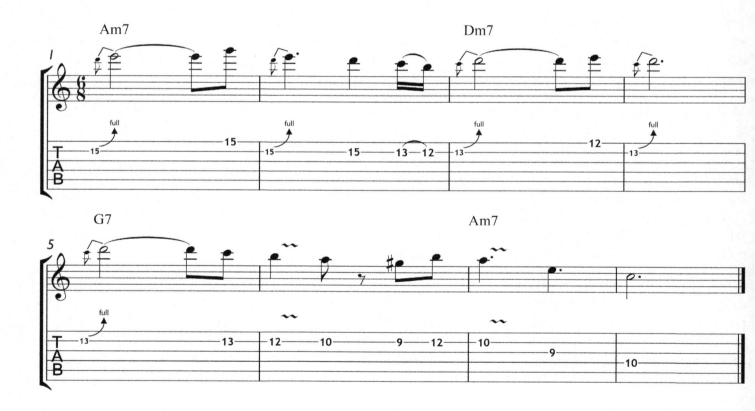

Long, sustained bends fuel Example 17b and this is a great exercise in timing, pitching and releasing bends. When you've learned the phrase, try varying the points at which you bring the bends up to pitch and listen to the effect a long, drawn out bend creates. You must anticipate the bend at the start of bar two, so open this lick with the first finger at the 9th fret, the third finger at the 12th fret of the B string, and the first finger at the 10th fret. You are now set up for a stable third finger bend at the 12th.

Example 17b

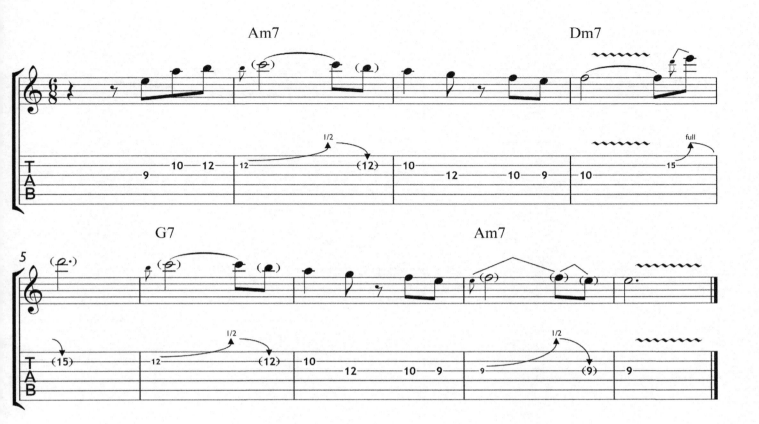

Moore's knowledge of jazz enabled him to transcend basic minor/major pentatonic vocabulary to play more sophisticated ideas. This example opens with an E Minor arpeggio (E, G, B) superimposed against both Am7 and Dm7 chords. This simple idea adds a lot of colour, implying Am9 and Dm6 chords. If you are playing with an overdriven tone, be careful with your picking dynamics on these arpeggios. Pick too hard and an excess of overdrive will create a muddy blend of notes. Relax the picking, or even better, work the volume knob to decrease/increase the amount of gain.

Example 17c

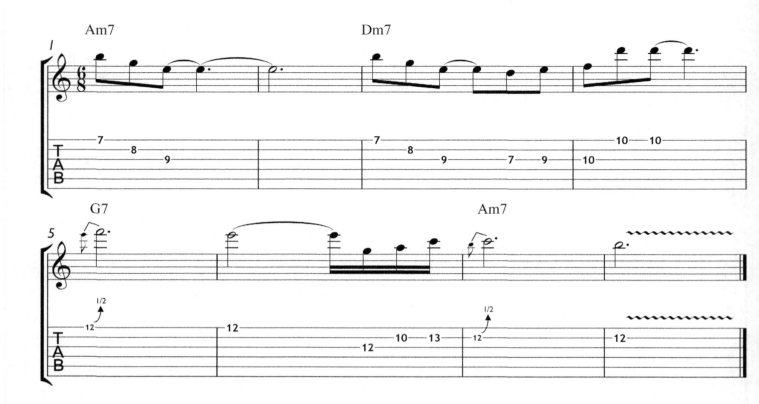

Example 17d is a busier Moore-style line, relying on arpeggios to outline the underlying chords. The phrase in bar one combines the A Minor Pentatonic scale with an Am7 arpeggio (A, C, E, G). When we hit the IV chord (Dm7) a superimposed FMaj7 arpeggio (F, A, C, E) outlines the chord tones of Dm7 and adds the 9th of the chord for color. In bar one, use a first finger barre for the notes at the 5th fret, then play the notes at the 7th fret of the D and A strings with the third and second fingers respectively.

82

Example 17d

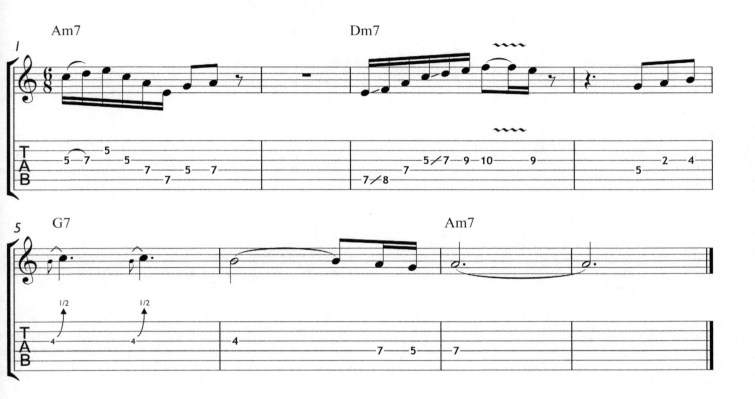

Example 17e is a good lesson in how knowing your scales all over the fretboard gives you much greater control – not only of *what* you say but *how* and *where* you say it. While not as technically challenging as previous lines, the precise use of bends and vibrato come under the microscope in this intro. Open the lick by using the first finger at the 2nd fret of the D and G strings. For a cleaner sound, try not to barre and instead "roll" the index finger from the D to G string.

Example 17e

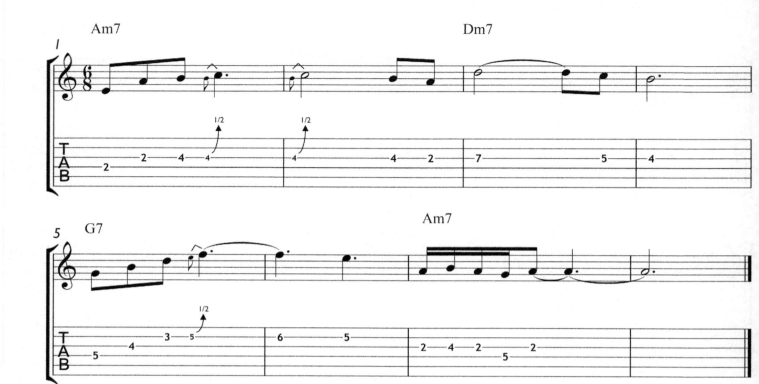

Chapter Eighteen: Jeff Beck

Geoffrey Arnold Jeff Beck was born in 1944 in a suburb of London, England, and began playing guitar in his teens with a borrowed instrument. Like several other English guitarists of his generation, he attended an Art College while becoming actively involved with different local bands. Influenced by players like Les Paul and guitarist Cliff Gallup's recordings with Gene Vincent and The Blue Caps, Beck also listened intently to Blues players such as B.B. King. In his early years, he became something of a session guitarist before joining his first notable group, The Yardbirds, in 1965, where he replaced Eric Clapton on the recommendation of Jimmy Page.

Beck played with The Yardbirds for just under two years and recorded one studio album with them in 1966, but was eventually fired during a US tour for missing gigs and having a rather temperamental attitude. Upon leaving this group, Beck recruited Jimmy Page and Keith Moon to record *Beck's Bolero* which was followed by two solo singles: *Hi Ho Silver Lining* and *Tallyman*. His next group was The Jeff Beck Group, which included a young Rod Stewart on vocals. They recorded two albums, *Truth* (1968) and *Beck-Ola* (1969), before disbanding in July 1969. Beck then teamed up with drummer Carmine Appice and bassist Tim Bogart to form a rock power-trio, but the project was interrupted after Beck was badly injured in a car crash. He later returned to work with them before the group dissolved in 1974.

By the mid-1970s Beck had produced two instrumental albums (*Blow by Blow* and *Wired*), that showcased his unique approach to the electric guitar in a series of stunning instrumentals, influenced by the jazz-rock movement prevalent at the time. These are still considered among his best recordings. He released three studio albums in the 1980s and was involved with numerous different studio projects and guest appearances.

Since the 1990s Beck has steadily produced high-quality solo albums at a much higher rate than in past decades. He still tours regularly and is widely regarded as one of rock's greatest and most individual-sounding guitar players.

Jeff Beck has, at various points in his career, used both Gibson Les Pauls and Fender Telecasters, but it is undoubtedly his long association with the Fender Stratocaster that has given him his unrivalled reputation. Fender's Custom Shop now produce a Jeff Beck model made to his exact specifications. His Stratocasters are modified to allow considerable up-pull on the tremolo arm, giving Beck the ability to create sounds only dreamed of by other players. His amplifiers are generally Marshalls or Fenders, and although he does use some effects, his hands and guitars create most of his tones and radical sound changes.

Beck's playing style is utterly unique, and he frequently manipulates the tremolo arm to produce tones reminiscent of a slide guitarist or pedal steel player. An excellent example of his tremolo arm technique is the track *Where Were You* from the 1989 album *Guitar Shop*. He also frequently employs harmonics (both natural and artificial) to great effect within a melody line and favours volume swells and fast tremolo picking/right-hand tapping.

In contrast to many mainstream rock guitarists, Beck constantly manipulates the guitar's volume and tone controls to change the tone of his instrument while performing. His slide playing and tremolo arm use is astonishingly accurate in terms of intonation, and he has used it to recreate non-Western melodies on guitar such as on the track *Nadia* from his 2001 album, *You Had It Coming*.

Suggested Listening:

Truth – Jeff Beck Group

Guitar Shop

Blow by Blow

Emotion and Commotion

Jeff Beck often uses bluesy/rock flavoured riffs as backdrops to his solos. This one isn't too challenging, so focus on getting up to the required speed with tight timing, some swing, and controlled alternate picking throughout.

Example 18a

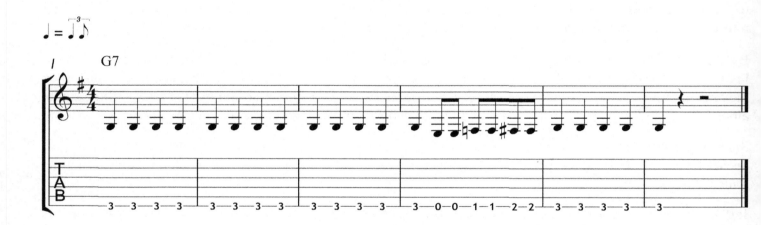

You can play Example 18b with a pick, but Beck typically alternates his picking hand thumb and first finger for picking duties. To play the country-esque lick in bar two, use a reinforced third finger for the bend at the 14th fret, followed by the fourth finger at the 15th. Bars 3-4 show how his rhythmic phrasing can be quite erratic. Bar five demonstrates his sometimes unusual fretting, so use the fourth finger on the A string and the first finger on the D string here.

Example 18b

Playing triplets at this tempo is challenging, so learn this lick slowly. In bar three it's tempting to place a first finger barre at the 15th fret, but this may result in the phrase sounding too muddy. In this instance it's better to move the first finger to each string rather than barring, so you have a first to second finger hammer-on from the 15th to 16th fret, followed by a first to third finger hammer-on from the 15th to 17th fret when you move to the B string.

Example 18c

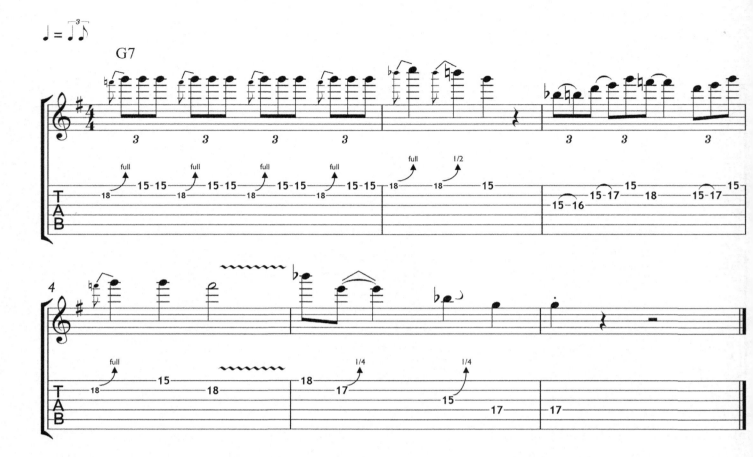

In this example the unpredicatable pattern of notes takes you into Beck's jazz/fusion style. Playing wider intervals breaks up the typical pentatonic box shape, but does look daunting. If you use the one-finger-per-fret rule, however, you can negotiate it easily.

Example 18d

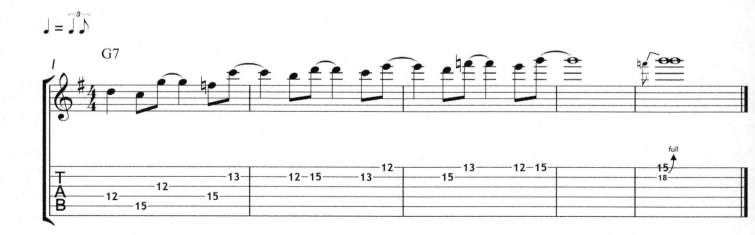

This last example focuses more on Beck's blues/rock approach. Play a partial barre for the notes at the 15th fret in bar two with the first finger, and use the third and fourth fingers for the notes that follow on the 17th and 15th frets respectively. Start bar three with the second finger at the 16th fret of the D string, then return to the A string, 17th fret, with the third finger. Finally, use the first finger for the notes at the 15th and 14th frets of the A string.

Example 18e

Chapter Nineteen: John Mayer

Like Eric Clapton, John Mayer is an artist who has found global stardom in the rock/pop world while keeping the blues prominent in much of what he does. Mayer has had chart topping hits but has still found time to release albums which focus more on his Jimi Hendrix and Stevie Ray Vaughan influences.

Born in Bridgeport, Connecticut, on October 17th, 1977, he took up guitar aged 13 when he was inspired by Marty McFly's famous performance scene in the film *Back To The Future*. He soon discovered Stevie Ray Vaughan which led him to B.B. King, Buddy Guy, Freddie and Albert King, and Lightnin' Hopkins amongst others.

He had a brief tenure as a student at the famous Berklee College of Music, but dropped out to pursue his career as a singer-songwriter. Signing with Columbia Records, Mayer's first two albums were firmly rooted in the mainstream with an acoustic pop/rock sound and he won the Grammy for Best Male Pop Vocal Performance in 2003. However, from this point he shifted his focus to the blues/rock he had grown up with, adapting his writing style and going on to perform alongside Eric Clapton, B.B. King, Buddy Guy and a raft of other legends.

Although he would return to the commercial sound of his earlier albums, the blues has always been very much at the fore. Mayer's blues is a great synthesis of his influences, so you'll hear elements of Clapton, B.B. King and Stevie Ray Vaughan wrapped up in his melodic approach.

Mayer is a master of creating hook-laden intro licks, perhaps more so than Eric Clapton. Listen to the intro of *Vultures* from the *Continuum* album and you'll hear how he can take a bluesy phrase and turn it into a commercial sounding melody with repetition and restraint.

Mayer is worth hearing for the great array of tones he conjures alone. A true gear hound, he has chopped and changed equipment all over the place. You'll generally see him with a Strat and a Dumble or Two Rock amplifier, which gives him a huge, powerful clean tone with a hint of overdrive when needed. He's a very touch sensitive and dynamic player and his choice of equipment really allows him to get the widest possible tonal range in his playing.

Over the years he has had several signature model guitars released, most notably the John Mayer signature Fender Stratocaster and, more recently, the Paul Reed Smith Silver Sky. There have also been limited (and very expensive) amplifiers with Two Rock and Paul Reed Smith.

John Mayer's blues playing can be quite challenging to copy as he combines so many elements of the greats. He has drawn from B.B. King's vibrato and ryhthms, Clapton's more rock-based approach and Stevie Ray Vaughan's attack and speed. He is a hugely versatile musician and has worked alongside artists from a wide variety of genres, from jazz legends like Herbie Hancock and guitarists Charlie Hunter and John Scofield, to rappers Kanye West and Common. Live, he has appeared with everyone from The Rolling Stones to The Grateful Dead.

Recommended Listening

Paradise Valley

Continuum

Room for Squares

Where the Light Is: John Mayer Live in Los Angeles

Mayer's music covers various blues styles, and in these examples I've opted to cover his approach on a blues with a funky, swing feel.

Mayer's jazz-influenced chord vocabulary means his playing uses more sophisticated voicings than many other blues players. Play this example with a relaxed, loose picking hand wrist to achieve the desired "bounce" off the strings. Lightly release the fretting hand fingers after you strike each chord to get that punctuated staccato sound.

Example 19a

This example is built around the F Minor Pentatonic scale, but the jumpy rhythms and tempo make it a great alternate picking workout. Keep the picking wrist relaxed and loose so you can pick every note without tensing up. In the second bar, use the third finger on the 2nd fret of the A string, then slide it up to the 3rd fret as this maintains the clean one-finger-per-fret approach to position playing.

Example 19b

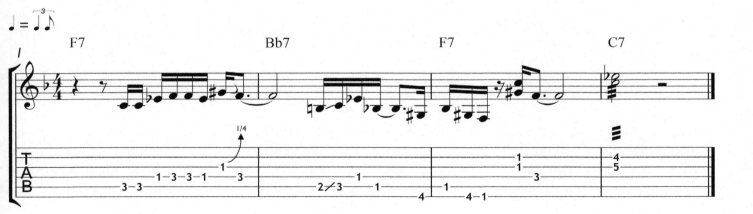

Here the F Minor Pentatonic scale has a brief addition of the 9th (via the open G string in bar three). This lick features two rapid phrases that are a great workout for the fretting hand. Instead of playing legato, copy Mayer's alternate picking approach on a line like this.

Example 19c

Bar three of this example showcases the Hendrix influence on Mayer's playing with double-stop ideas. Executing the hammer-ons and pull-offs within the double-stop can be a challenge, so try these fretting hand fingerings: use the second finger for the 16th fret on the B string, the first finger on the 15th fret of the G string, then hammer-on to the 17th fret with the third finger.

Example 19d

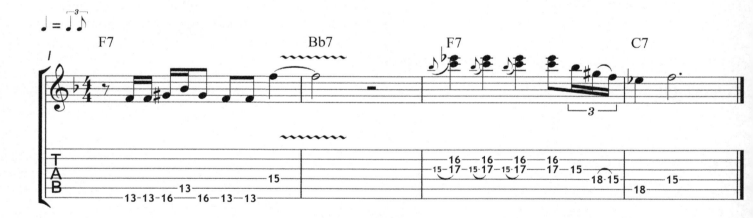

Mayer's country guitar influence results in him playing some fun licks with a strong major feel. This phrase is based around the F Major Pentatonic scale. To get that country sound, focus on playing the pre-bend and release cleanly in bar one. There is a small position shift in bar three, so use the third finger on the E string at both the 8th and 10th frets before returning the third finger to the 8th fret of the B string in the following bar.

Example 19e

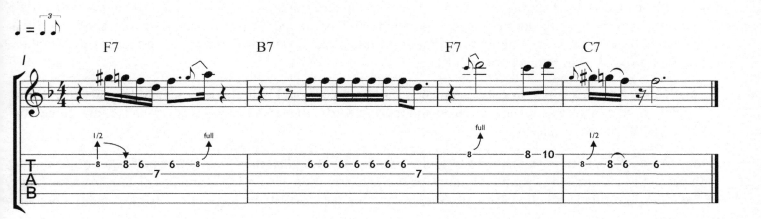

Chapter Twenty: Kenny Wayne Shepherd

Like Joe Bonamassa and Gary Moore, Kenny Wayne Shepherd is a blues artist who incorporates a harder rock sound into his playing. This does not mean that Shepherd has strayed from his roots, however, and he is still a consumate bluesman at heart. Taking up guitar at the age of 7, he was inspired by seeing Stevie Ray Vaughan perform and soon began to teach himself by ear.

By age 13 he was performing in public and soon inked a record deal with industry legend Irving Azoff. From this point on, Shepherd was releasing music and touring across the USA becoming a regular fixture in the Top 10 of the Billboard blues charts.

Kenny Wayne Shepherd is an example of today's younger blues players who combine scintillating technique with perfect blues phrasing. Some of today's new artists are often accused of being too distant from the heart of the blues, but this is not the case with Shepherd, who has worked alongside legends like Buddy Guy and B.B. King.

In 2007 he released a documentary series called *10 Days Out – Blues From The Backroads*, in which he sought out and jammed with elder blues legends including Clarence "Gatemouth" Brown, Hubert Sumlin and Honeyboy Edwards, among others. While Shepherd plays with a rock-inflected technique, he is firmly rooted in the blues and has a great reverence for the music and its pioneers.

He has managed to create a successful career within blues, becoming a regular presence in the Top 10 of the Billboard blues charts. Part of his success may be due to the fact that he hasn't fallen into the trap of being a typical blues guitarist/vocalist – i.e. someone who is a great guitarist but a sub-standard vocalist. Rather, he often works with Noah Hunt, who fulfils the role of lead vocalist and frontman when needed. Working with a harder blues/rock sound has led to crossover success and he has opened for various rock acts (and consequently large audiences) like Van Halen.

Kenny Wayne Shepherd mostly plays Fender Stratocasters and in 2008, the company released the KWS signature Strat. He has used various amps during his career but today he is trying to lower the onstage volume, so you'll see him with a Fender 1964 Vibroverb reissue, a Fender Supersonic Twin and a Fender Deluxe reissue that has been modified by Alexander Dumble. He runs these three amps together, which helps him get a huge tone at comparatively low volumes.

His pedalboard is a bit more elaborate than most in the genre and incorporates Univibe, Octavia, Chorus, Delay and various overdrives/boosts including a handwired Ibanez Tubescreamer.

Recommended Listening

Trouble Is…

Ledbetter Heights

How I Go

Shepherd's solos and intro licks can be technically challenging, with uptempo, burning licks, so these examples may take some work. He'll often go beyond the standard box shapes to play the whole neck, and his powerful attack and huge, Dumble-driven tones make him a joy to study.

This first example is a good alternate picking workout and showcases Shepherd's typically tight, clean rhythmic phrasing. From the end of bar three, the one-finger-per-fret rule will work well.

Example 20a

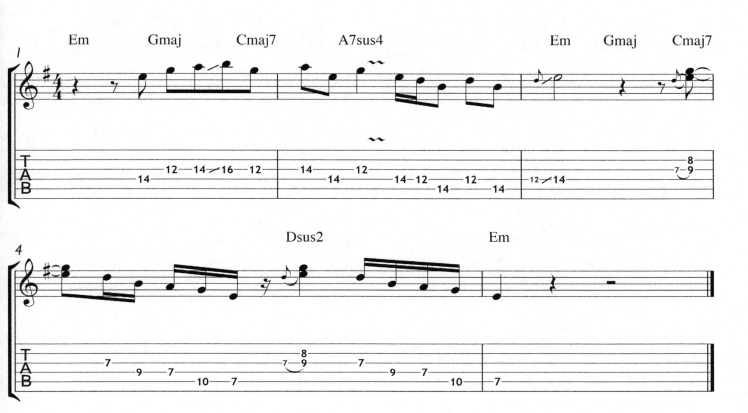

Bring life to the double-stops in bars 1-2 using heavy vibrato, a heavy picking hand attack and fretting hand muting. Use your second and third fingers respectively to hold down the notes at the 15th and 16th frets of the B and G strings. Lightly place your first finger across the strings behind these notes to mute the other strings you will be catching with the picking hand. These muted notes are part of the effect.

Example 20b

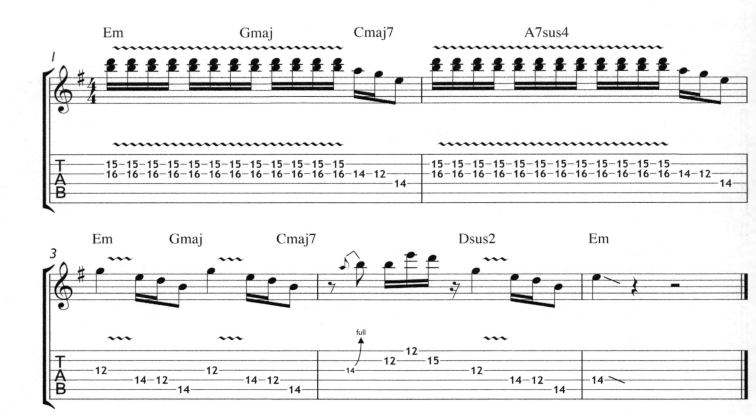

This example uses the E Natural Minor scale (E, F#, G, A, B, C, D) to create a melodic phrase with a cohesive, consistent rhythm that sounds more like a melody than a lick. Using rhythm in this way is a great tool, especially as far as intros are concerned, where you want to express strong melodic ideas rather than just play licks.

Example 20c

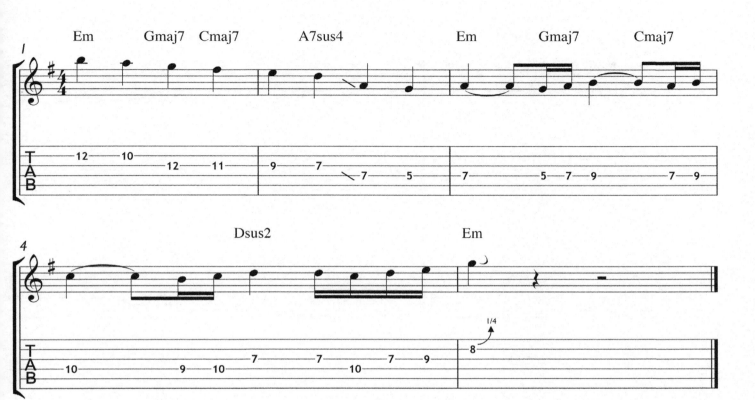

Shepherd often plays technical phrases, as in bar one of Example 20d, with a precision more commonly found in rock players. You can use a first finger barre at the 12th fret of the E and B strings, but this can cause some defintion to be lost, so it's better to rapidly move the first finger from the E string to the B string each time, and this should be done when the third finger lands on the 15th fret of the B string.

Example 20d

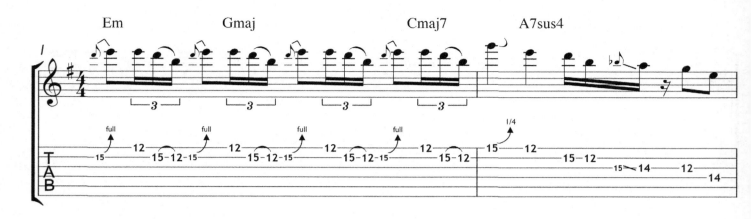

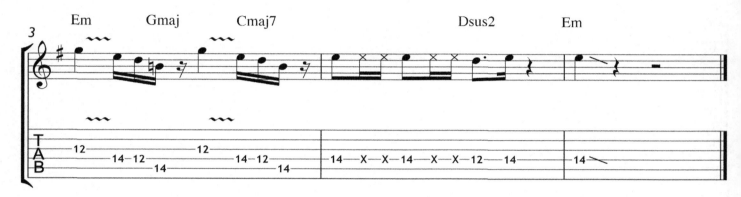

The main challenge in this final Shepherd-style lick is bar three's demanding triplet rhythm on the "and" of each beat. Play this using the third finger for any notes on the 17th fret, the first finger on the 15th fret, and the fourth finger on the 19th fret. I've suggested an alternate picking pattern. Practice this slowly on repeat and you'll soon program it into muscle memory.

Example 20e

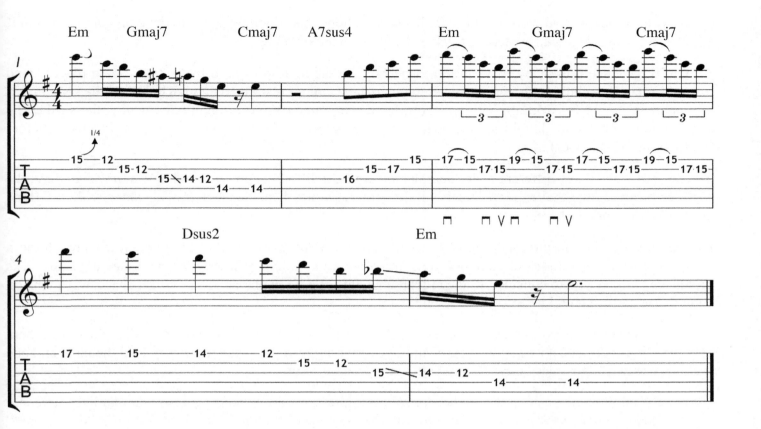

Conclusion

Thank you for buying and working through this book. I hope that it will help you to develop your confidence, whether playing along with a backing track or leading a band on a gig.

As you'll have seen, in many ways the intro phrase is a distillation of an artist's style. Some players tend towards a flashy, technique-driven intro, while others take a more restrained approach, letting the song unfurl around them. Some are working within a short, fixed timeframe of four or eight bars, while others (like The Three Kings) are able to play for as long as they want, using the intro to set the scene and build tension before finally bringing the vocal in.

You have also seen how different styles and meters require a different approach and how a time signature like 12/8 can bring its own challenges. Likewise, if the song is swung, then you need to swing along with it. T-Bone Walker is your mentor here.

It's tempting to view an intro as a short solo – a brief collection of licks – but of course it is so much more than that, so it's a good idea to compose your intros before jamming or hitting the bandstand. Writing licks in this way allows you to consider all the crucial elements of a good phrase: note choice, space, tone, tension and release, phrasing and more.

Finally, watch as much live footage of all these players as you can, as this is where you will see and hear them play most honestly. See how in control they are of everything they do; watch how they lead the band and cue sections or signal dynamics changes, or just how they start a song.

Ultimately, an intro lick can either be the start of a song or the start of your solo, so take the licks here and reshape them to create your own. Next time you are out with the band, you'll now be able to say, "Follow me!"

Stuart Ryan

Bath, UK, 2021

Printed in Great Britain
by Amazon

42545580R00057